P9-DVU-481

D0037612

cook's library

Pasta & Italian

cook's library

Pasta &
Italian

p

This is a Parragon Publishing Book
This edition published in 2004

Parragon Publishing
Queen Street House
4 Queen Street
Bath BA1 1HE, UK

Copyright © Parragon 2002

All rights reserved. No part of this publication may be reproduced,
stored in a retrieval system, or transmitted, in any form or by any means,
electronic, mechanical, photocopying, recordings, or otherwise, without
the prior permission of the copyright holder.

ISBN: 0-75259-953-4

Printed in China

NOTE

Cup measurements in this book are for American cups. This book
uses imperial and metric measurements. Follow the same units of
measurement throughout; do not mix imperial and metric. All spoon
measurements are level: teaspoons are assumed to be 5 ml,
and tablespoons are assumed to be 15 ml. Unless otherwise stated,
milk is assumed to be full fat, eggs and individual vegetables such
as potatoes are medium, and pepper is freshly ground black pepper.

The times given for each recipe are an approximate guide only because
the preparation times may differ according to the techniques used by
different people and the cooking times may vary as a result of the type
of oven used. The preparation times include chilling and marinating
times, where appropriate.

Recipes using raw or very lightly cooked eggs should be avoided
by infants, the elderly, pregnant women, convalescents, and anyone
suffering from an illness.

Contents

Introduction

Italian food, including the many pasta dishes, pizzas, and risottos, is enjoyed all around the world. This inspirational cookbook aims to bring a little bit of Italy into your kitchen!

Glorious sunlight, spectacular beaches, luscious countryside, rugged mountains, world-famous museums and art galleries, elegant designer shops, picturesque villages, and magnificent cities—if this were not enough, Italy also boasts one of the longest and finest culinary traditions in the whole of Europe.

The ancient Romans loved good food and plenty of it, vying with each other to produce increasingly lavish and outlandish banquets. One of the earliest cookbooks was written by Apicius, a Roman gourmet in the first century, though some of its recipes might not appeal to us today! Overseas trade, as the Roman Empire expanded, brought new ingredients, and agriculture began to flourish at home. And wine production was just as prodigious as it is today.

With the collapse of the Roman Empire, the diet of the region returned to plainer fare, relying mainly on the wealth of cereals, fruit, and vegetables that could be cultivated on the fertile plains. However, with the Renaissance, an interest in and enthusiasm for fine food revived and, once again, wealthy families presided over extravagant banquets.

Italian pastry cooks were valued throughout the courts of Europe and were generally acknowledged as the best in the world. When Catherine de Medici went to Paris to marry the future King Henri II, she took an army of Italian cooks with her and changed French culinary traditions irrevocably. A new middle class developed who also took an interest in eating well, creating a bourgeois cuisine characterized by fresh flavors and simple, unsauced dishes. The poor, of course, continued with their peasant subsistence.

The very finest produce and freshest ingredients still characterize Italian cuisine as a whole. Although modern transportation makes it possible for more exotic ingredients to travel across the world, Italian cooking still centers on home-grown produce. Over 60 percent of the land is devoted to crops and pasture. With a climate that ranges from very cold in the Alps and Apennines to semitropical along the coast of the Ligurian Sea, the range of produce is extensive: olives, oranges, lemons, figs, grapes, pomegranates, almonds, wheat, potatoes, tomatoes, sugar beet, corn, and rice.

Livestock includes cattle and buffalo, sheep, goats, pigs, and chickens. In a single year, Italy produces nearly 6.5 million metric tonnes of wine, nearly 2.5 million tonnes of olives, about 500,000 tonnes of olive oil, over 4.5 million tonnes of tomatoes and 120 million chickens. An impressive amount, you'll agree!

The introduction to this book continues to explore Italy, region by region, to discover the different types of food that are identified with specific areas of the country. Seasonal ingredients are also examined to provide the reader with an insight into the type of produce used by the very discerning people of Italy.

Ragu Sauce

3 tbsp olive oil

3 tbsp butter

2 large onions, chopped

4 celery stalks, thinly sliced

6 oz/175 g bacon, chopped

2 garlic cloves, chopped

1 lb/450 g ground lean beef

2 tbsp tomato paste

1 tbsp flour

2 cups canned chopped tomatoes

⅔ cup beef bouillon

⅔ cup red wine

2 tsp dried oregano

½ tsp freshly grated nutmeg

salt and pepper

1 Heat the oil and butter in a pan over a medium heat. Add the onions, celery, and bacon and pan fry for 5 minutes, stirring.

2 Stir in the garlic and ground beef and cook, stirring until the meat has lost its redness. Lower the heat and cook for 10 minutes, stirring.

3 Increase the heat to medium, stir in the tomato paste and the flour and cook for 1–2 minutes. Stir in the tomatoes, bouillon, and wine and bring to the boil. Season and stir in the oregano and nutmeg. Cover and simmer for 45 minutes, stirring occasionally. The sauce is now ready to use.

Basic Pasta Dough

1 lb 4 oz/550 g durum wheat flour

4 eggs, lightly beaten

1 tbsp olive oil

salt

1 Lightly flour a work surface. Sift the flour with a pinch of salt into a mound. Make a well in the center and add the eggs and oil.

2 Using a fork or your fingertips, gradually work the mixture until the ingredients are combined. Knead vigorously for 10–15 minutes.

3 Set the dough aside to rest for 25 minutes, before rolling it out as thinly and evenly as possible, and cutting to the required shape.

Pasta may be colored and flavored with extra ingredients that are usually added with the beaten egg:

Black	add 1 tsp squid or cuttlefish ink.
Green	add 4 oz/115 g well-drained, cooked spinach.
Purple	work 1 large, cooked beetroot in a food processor and add with 2 oz/55 g extra flour.
Red	add 2 tbsp tomato paste.

Regional Cooking

To talk about Italian cuisine is somewhat misleading, as it is not a single entity. The country has been united only since March 17, 1861 and Italians still have a powerful sense of their regional identity. Regional cuisine is a source of pride and considerable competition. Sicilians are dismissed as *mangimaccaroni* (pasta eaters), while they express their contempt for Neapolitan cooking with the term *mangiafoglie* (vegetable eaters). Each region bases its cuisine on local ingredients, so the best ham comes from the area where pigs are raised, fish and seafood feature in coastal regions, butter is used in dishes from the north of Italy where there is dairy farming, while olive oil is characteristic of southern recipes.

Abruzzi & Molise

This was once a single region and although it has now been divided into two separate provinces, they remain closely associated. Located in northern Italy to the east of Rome, the area is wellknown for its high-quality cured meats and cheese. The cuisine is traditional and also features lamb and fish and seafood in the coastal areas. Peperoncino, a tiny, fiery hot, dried red chile, is from Abruzzi.

Basilicata

If the Italian peninsula looks like a boot, Basilicata is located on the arch of the foot. The landscape is rugged and inhospitable, with much of the region being over 6,500 feet/2,000 meters above sea level. It is hardly surprising, therefore, that the cuisine is warming and filling, featuring substantial soups in particular. Cured meats, pork, lamb, and game are typical ingredients and freshwater fish are abundant in the more mountainous areas.

Calabria

In the south, on Italy's toe, Calabria is a region of dramatic contrasts—superb beaches and towering mountains. Excellent fish and seafood typify the local cuisine, which is well known for its swordfish and tuna dishes. Fruit and vegetables are abundant, particularly oranges, lemons, eggplants, and olives. Like other southern regions, desserts are a specialty, often based on local figs, honey or almonds.

Campania

Naples on the west coast is the home of pizza, now known across the world from Sydney to New York, and the region bases many of its other dishes on the wonderful sun-ripened tomatoes grown locally. Fish and seafood feature strongly in the Neapolitan diet and robust herb-flavored stews, redolent with garlic, are popular. Pastries and fruit desserts are also characteristic.

Emilia-Romagna

A central Italian province, Emilia-Romagna's capital is the beautiful medieval city of Bologna, nicknamed *la grassa*, the fat city, and home to some of the best restaurants in the country.

A gourmet paradise, the region is famous for Parmesan cheese and Parma ham from Parma, balsamic vinegar from the area around Modena, cotechino, mortadella, and other cured meats and, of course, spaghetti alla bolognese. Butter, cream, and other dairy products feature in the fine food of the region and a wide range of pasta dishes is popular.

Lazio

Capital of the region and the country, Rome is a cosmopolitan and sophisticated city with some of the best restaurants—and ice cream parlors—in Europe. Fruit and vegetables are abundant and lamb and veal dishes are typical of the region, which is famous for saltimbocca, or "jump in the mouth", so named because it is so delicious. Here, they have perfected the art of preparing high-quality ingredients in simple, but delicious ways that retain the individual flavors.

A Roman specialty is *supplì al telefono* (telephone wires)—mozzarella cheese wrapped in balls of cooked rice and deep-fried. The mozzarella is stringy, hence the name of the dish.

Liguria

A northern province with a long coastline, Liguria is well known for its superb fish and seafood. It is also said to produce the best basil in Italy and it is where pesto sauce was first invented. The ancient port of Genoa was one of the first places in Europe to import Asian spices and highly seasoned dishes are still characteristic of this area.

Lombardy

An important rice-growing region in northwest Italy, this is the home of risotto and there are probably as many variations of this dish as there are cooks. Lombardy is credited with the invention of butter, as well as mascarpone cheese. Vegetable soups, stews, and pot roasts are characteristic of this region. Bresaola, cured raw beef, is a local specialty that is often served wrapped around a locally produced soft goat's cheese.

Marche

With its long coastline and high mountains, this region is blessed with both abundant seafood and game. Pasta, pork, and olives also feature and methods of preparation are even more elaborate than those of neighboring Umbria.

Piedmont

On the borders of France and Switzerland, Piedmont in the northwest is strongly influenced by its neighbors. A fertile, arable region, it is well known for rice, polenta, and gnocchi and is said to grow the finest onions in Italy. Gorgonzola, one of the world's greatest cheeses, comes from this region although, sadly, the village that gave it its name has now been subsumed by the urban sprawl of Milan. Piedmontese garlic is said to be the best in Italy and the local white truffles are a gourmet's dream.

Puglia

On the heel of Italy, this region produces excellent olives, herbs, vegetables, and fruit, particularly melons and figs. Fish and seafood are abundant, because of its proximity to the coast and fishing ports, and the region is known for its oyster and mussel dishes. Calzone, a sort of inside out pizza, was invented here.

Sardinia

This Mediterranean island is famous for its luxurious desserts and extravagant pastries, many of them featuring honey, nuts, and home-grown fruit. Hardly surprisingly, fish and seafood— tuna, eel, mullet, sea bass, lobster, and mussels—are central to Sardinian cuisine and spit-roasted suckling pig is the national dish served on feast days. Sardo is a mild-tasting pecorino cheese also produced in Sardinia.

Sicily

Like their southern neighbors, Sicilians have a sweet tooth, which they indulge with superb cakes, desserts, and ice cream, often incorporating locally grown almonds, pistachios, and citrus fruits. Pasta dishes are an important part of the diet and fish and seafood, including tuna, swordfish and mussels, feature prominently.

Trentino Alto-Adige

A mountainous region in the northeast, Trentino has been strongly influenced by its Austrian neighbor. Smoked sausage and dumplings are characteristic of the region, which is also well known for its filled pasta dishes.

Tuscany

The fertile plains of Tuscany are ideal for farming and the region produces superb fruit and vegetables. Cattle are raised here and both steak and veal dishes feature on the Tuscan menu, together with a wide range of game. Tripe is a local specialty and Panforte di Siena, a traditional Christmas cake made with honey and nuts, comes from the city of Siena. A grain known as farro is grown almost exclusively in Tuscany, where it is used to make a nourishing soup.

Umbria

Pork, lamb, game, and freshwater fish, prepared and served simply,

but deliciously, characterize the excellent cuisine of the region. Fragrant black truffles are a feature and Umbrian cooking makes good use of its high-quality olive oil. Umbria is also famous for *imbrecciata*, a hearty soup made with lentils, garbanzo beans, and navy beans.

Veneto and Friuli

An intensively farmed area in the northeast of Italy, this region produces cereals and almost 20 percent of the country's wine. Polenta and risotto feature in the cuisine, as well as an extensive range of fish and seafood. *Risi e bisi*, rice and peas, is a dish which was served every year at the Doge's banquet in Venice to honor the city's patron saint, Mark.

Basic Recipes

These recipes form the basis of several of the dishes contained throughout this book. Many of these basic recipes can be made in advance and stored in the refrigerator until required.

Basic Tomato Sauce

2 tbsp olive oil

1 small onion, chopped

1 garlic clove, chopped

2 cups canned chopped tomatoes

2 tbsp chopped parsley

1 tsp dried oregano

2 bay leaves

2 tbsp tomato paste

1 tsp sugar

salt and pepper

1 Heat the oil in a pan over a medium heat and pan-fry the onion for 2–3 minutes or until translucent. Add the garlic and pan-fry for 1 minute.

2 Stir in the chopped tomatoes, parsley, oregano, bay leaves, tomato paste, sugar, and salt and pepper to taste.

3 Bring the sauce to the boil, then simmer, uncovered, for 15–20 minutes or until the sauce has reduced by half. Taste the sauce and adjust the seasoning if necessary. Discard the bay leaves just before serving.

Béchamel Sauce

1¼ cups milk

2 bay leaves

3 whole cloves

1 small onion

¼ cup butter

6 tbsp flour

1¼ cups light cream

large pinch of freshly grated nutmeg

salt and pepper

1 Pour the milk into a small pan and add the bay leaves. Press the cloves into the onion, add to the pan and bring the milk to the boil. Remove the pan from the heat and set aside to cool.

2 Strain the milk into a jug and rinse the pan. Melt the butter in the pan and stir in the flour. Stir for 1 minute, then gradually pour in the milk, stirring constantly. Cook the sauce for 3 minutes, then pour in the cream and bring it to a boil. Remove from the heat and season with nutmeg, salt and pepper to taste.

Lamb Sauce

2 tbsp olive oil

1 large onion, sliced

2 celery stalks, thinly sliced

1 lb/450 g lean lamb, ground

3 tbsp tomato paste

5½ oz bottled sun-dried tomatoes, drained and chopped

1 tsp dried oregano

1 tbsp red wine vinegar

⅔ cup chicken bouillon

salt and pepper

1 Heat the oil in a skillet over a medium heat and fry the onion and celery until the onion is translucent, about 3 minutes. Add the lamb and pan-fry, stirring frequently, until it browns evenly.

2 Stir in the tomato paste, sun-dried tomatoes, oregano, vinegar, and bouillon. Season with salt and pepper to taste.

3 Bring the sauce to a boil and cook, uncovered, for 20 minutes or until the meat has absorbed the bouillon. Taste and adjust the seasoning if necessary.

Espagnole Sauce

2 tbsp butter

¼ cup all-purpose flour

1 tsp tomato paste

1 cup hot veal bouillon

1 tbsp Madeira

1½ tsp white wine vinegar

2 tbsp olive oil

2 strips bacon, diced

3 tbsp diced carrot

3 tbsp diced onion

3 tbsp diced celery

3 tbsp sliced leek

2 tbsp diced fennel

1 fresh thyme sprig

1 bay leaf

1 Melt the butter in a pan, add the flour and cook, stirring, until lightly colored. Add the tomato paste, then stir in the hot veal bouillon, Madeira, and white wine vinegar and cook for 2 minutes.

2 Heat the oil in a separate pan, add the bacon, carrot, onion, celery, leek, fennel, thyme sprig, and bay leaf and pan-fry until the vegetables have softened. Remove the vegetables from the pan with a slotted spoon and drain thoroughly. Add the vegetables to the sauce and leave to simmer for 4 hours, stirring occasionally. Strain the sauce before using.

Cheese Sauce

2 tbsp butter

1 tbsp flour

1 cup + 2 tbsp milk

2 tbsp light cream

pinch of freshly grated nutmeg

½ cup grated sharp colby cheese

1 tbsp freshly grated Parmesan cheese

salt and pepper

1 Melt the butter in a pan, stir in the flour and cook for 1 minute. Gradually pour in the milk, stirring all the time. Stir in the cream and season the sauce with nutmeg, salt and pepper to taste.

2 Simmer the sauce for 5 minutes to reduce, then remove it from the heat and stir in the cheeses. Stir until the cheeses have melted and blended into the sauce.

Italian Red Wine Sauce

⅝ cup Brown Bouillon (see page 16)

⅔ cup Espagnole Sauce (see left)

½ cup red wine

2 tbsp red wine vinegar

4 tbsp chopped shallots

1 bay leaf

1 thyme sprig

pepper

1 First make a demiglace sauce: combine the Brown Bouillon and Espagnole Sauce in a pan and heat for 10 minutes, stirring occasionally.

2 Meanwhile, put the red wine, red wine vinegar, shallots, bay leaf, and thyme in a pan, bring to a boil and reduce by three-quarters.

3 Strain the demiglace sauce and add to the pan containing the Red Wine Sauce and leave to simmer for 20 minutes, stirring occasionally. Season with pepper to taste and strain the sauce before using.

Brown Bouillon

2 lb/900 g veal bones and shin of beef

1 leek, sliced

1 onion, chopped

1 celery stalk, sliced

1 carrot, sliced

1 bouquet garni

²/₃ cup white wine vinegar

1 thyme sprig

7½ cups cold water

1 Roast the veal bones and shin of beef in their own juices in the oven for 40 minutes.

2 Transfer the bones to a large pan and add the leeks, onion, celery, carrots, bouquet garni, white wine vinegar, and thyme and cover with the cold water. Leave to simmer over a very low heat for about 3 hours. Strain and blot the fat from the surface with paper towels before using.

Fish Bouillon

2 lb/900 g non-oily fish pieces, such as heads, tails, trimmings and bones

²/₃ cup white wine

1 onion, chopped

1 carrot, sliced

1 celery stalk, sliced

4 black peppercorns

1 bouquet garni

7½ cups water

1 Put the fish pieces, wine, onion, carrot, celery, black peppercorns, bouquet garni, and water in a large pan and leave to simmer for 30 minutes, stirring occasionally. Strain and blot the fat from the surface of the bouillon with paper towels before using.

Italian Cheese Sauce

2 tbsp butter

¼ cup all-purpose flour

1¼ cups hot milk

pinch of nutmeg

pinch of dried thyme

2 tbsp white wine vinegar

3 tbsp heavy cream

½ cup grated mozzarella cheese

½ cup Parmesan cheese

1 tsp English mustard

2 tbsp sour cream

salt and pepper

1 Melt the butter in a pan and then stir in the flour. Cook, stirring, over a low heat until the roux is light in color and crumbly in texture. Stir in the hot milk and cook, stirring, for 15 minutes, until thick and smooth.

2 Add the nutmeg, thyme, white wine vinegar, and season to taste. Stir in the cream and mix well.

3 Stir in the cheeses, mustard, and sour cream and mix until the cheeses have melted and blended into the sauce.

How to Use This Book

Each recipe contains a wealth of useful information, including a breakdown of nutritional quantities, preparation and cooking times, and level of difficulty. All of this information is explained in detail below.

A full-color photograph of the finished dish.

The ingredients for each recipe are listed in the order that they are used.

The nutritional information provided for each recipe is per serving or per portion. Optional ingredients, variations or serving suggestions have not been included in the calculations.

The method is clearly explained with step-by-step instructions that are easy to follow.

Cook's tips provide useful information regarding ingredients or cooking techniques.

17

PASTA & ITALIAN

The Italian name for this dish, Saltimbocca, means "jump into the mouth" because it is so delicious. The stuffed rolls are quick and easy to make.

Saltimbocca

SERVES 4

4 turkey fillets or 4 veal escalopes, about 1 lb/450 g in total
4 oz/115 g Parma ham
8 fresh sage leaves
1 tbsp olive oil
1 onion, finely chopped
¼ cup white wine
¼ cup chicken bouillon

1 Place the turkey or veal between sheets of waxed paper. Pound the meat with a meat mallet or the end of a rolling pin to flatten it slightly. Cut each escalope in half.

2 Trim the prosciutto to fit each piece of turkey or veal and place over the meat. Lay a sage leaf on top. Roll up the escalopes and secure with a wooden toothpick.

3 Heat the oil in a skillet and cook the onion for 3–4 minutes. Add the turkey or veal rolls to the pan and cook for 5 minutes, or until brown all over.

4 Pour the wine and bouillon into the pan and let simmer for 15 minutes if using turkey, and 20 minutes for veal, or until tender. Serve immediately.

NUTRITION
Calories 303; Sugars 0.3 g; Protein 29 g; Carbohydrate 1 g; Fat 17 g; Saturates 1 g

⭐⭐⭐ moderate
15 mins
25–30 mins

COOK'S TIP
If using turkey rather than veal, watch it carefully as turkey tends to turn dry very quickly if overcooked.

⭐ The number of stars represents the difficulty of each recipe, ranging from very easy (1 star) to challenging (4 stars).

This amount of time represents the preparation of ingredients, including cooling, chilling and soaking times.

This represents the cooking time.

Soups

Soups are an important part of the Italian cuisine. They vary in consistency from light and delicate to hearty main meal soups. Texture is always apparent—Italians rarely serve smooth soups. Some may be partially puréed but the identity of the ingredients is never entirely obliterated. There are regional characteristics, too. In the north, soups are often based on rice, while in Tuscany, thick bean- or bread-based soups are popular. Tomato, garlic, and pasta soups are typical of the south. Minestrone is known worldwide but the best-known version probably comes from Milan. However, all versions are full of vegetables and are delicious and satisfying. Fish soups also abound in one guise or another, and most of these are village specialties, so the variety is unlimited and always bursting in flavor.

This soup is best made with white onions, which have a milder flavor than the more usual brown variety. If you cannot get hold of them, try using large Spanish onions instead.

Tuscan Onion Soup

SERVES 4

½ cup pancetta ham, diced
1 tbsp olive oil
4 large white onions, thinly sliced into rings
3 garlic cloves, chopped
3¾ cups hot chicken or ham bouillon
4 slices ciabatta or other Italian bread
3 tbsp butter
¾ cup coarsely grated Gruyère or
    colby cheese
salt and pepper

1 Dry-fry the pancetta in a large pan for 3–4 minutes, or until it begins to brown. Remove the pancetta from the pan and set aside until required.

2 Add the oil to the pan and cook the onions and garlic over a high heat for 4 minutes. Reduce the heat, then cover and cook for 15 minutes, or until lightly caramelized.

3 Add the bouillon to the pan and bring to a boil. Reduce the heat and leave the mixture to simmer, covered, for about 10 minutes.

4 Toast the slices of ciabatta on both sides, under a preheated broiler, for 2–3 minutes, or until golden. Spread the ciabatta with butter and top with the Gruyère or colby cheese. Cut the bread into bite-size pieces.

5 Add the reserved pancetta to the soup and season to taste with salt and pepper. Pour into 4 soup bowls and top with the toasted bread.

NUTRITION

Calories *390*; Sugars *0g*; Protein *9g*;
Carbohydrate *15 g*; Fat *33 g*; Saturates *14 g*

⭐ very easy
🕐 5–10 mins
🕐 40–45 mins

 COOK'S TIP

Pancetta is similar to bacon, but it is air- and salt-cured for about 6 months. It is available from most delicatessens and some large supermarkets. If you cannot obtain pancetta, use unsmoked bacon instead.

A thick and creamy soup that is based on a traditional Tuscan recipe. If you use dried beans, the preparation and cooking times will be longer.

Tuscan Bean Soup

1   If you are using canned beans, drain them thoroughly and reserve the liquid. If you are using dried beans that have been soaked overnight, drain them thoroughly. Bring a large pan of water to a boil, add the beans and boil for 10 minutes. Cover the pan and simmer for a further 30 minutes or until tender. Drain the beans, reserving the cooking liquid.

2   Heat the oil in a large skillet and pan-fry the garlic for 2–3 minutes or until just beginning to brown.

3   Add the beans and 1²/₃ cup of the reserved liquid to the skillet, stirring. You may need to add a little water if there is insufficient liquid. Stir in the crumbled bouillon cube. Bring the mixture to a boil and then remove the skillet from the heat.

4   Place the bean mixture in a food processor and blend to form a smooth purée. Alternatively, mash the bean mixture to a smooth consistency. Season to taste with salt and pepper and stir in the milk.

5   Pour the soup back into the skillet and gently heat to just below boiling point. Stir in the oregano just before serving.

SERVES 4

2½ cups canned lima beans, or 8 oz/225 g dried lima beans, soaked overnight
1 tbsp olive oil
2 garlic cloves, crushed
1 vegetable or chicken bouillon cube, crumbled
²/₃ cup milk
2 tbsp chopped fresh oregano
salt and pepper

NUTRITION
Calories 250; Sugars 4 g; Protein 13 g;
Carbohydrate 29 g; Fat 10 g; Saturates 2 g

very easy

5 mins

10 mins

This thick, creamy soup has a wonderful, warming golden color. It is flavored with orange and thyme.

Orange, Thyme *and* Pumpkin Soup

SERVES 4

2 tbsp olive oil
2 medium onions, chopped
2 garlic cloves, chopped
2 lb/900 g pumpkin, peeled and cut into
  1-inch/2.5-cm chunks
6¼ cups boiling vegetable or chicken
  bouillon
finely grated rind and juice of 1 orange
3 tbsp fresh thyme, stalks removed
⅔ cup milk
salt and pepper
crusty bread, to serve

1 Heat the olive oil in a large pan. Add the onions to the pan and sauté for 3–4 minutes or until soft. Add the garlic and pumpkin and cook for a further 2 minutes, stirring well.

2 Add the boiling vegetable bouillon, orange rind and juice, and 2 tablespoons of the thyme to the pan. Leave to simmer, covered, for 20 minutes or until the pumpkin is tender.

3 Place the mixture in a food processor and blend until smooth. Alternatively, mash the mixture with a potato masher until smooth. Season to taste with salt and pepper.

4 Return the soup to the pan and add the milk. Reheat the soup for 3–4 minutes or until it is very hot but not boiling. Sprinkle with the remaining fresh thyme just before serving.

5 Divide the soup among 4 warm soup bowls and serve with lots of fresh crusty bread.

NUTRITION
Calories *111*; Sugars *4 g*; Protein *2 g*;
Carbohydrate *5 g*; Fat *6 g*; Saturates *2 g*

 very easy
 10 mins
🕐 35–40 mins

🍳 **COOK'S TIP**

Pumpkins are usually large vegetables. To make things a little easier, ask the store to cut a chunk off for you. Alternatively, make double the quantity and freeze the soup for up to 3 months.

This refreshing chilled soup is ideal on a hot day for al fresco dining.

Artichoke Soup

1 Heat the oil in a large pan and cook the chopped onion and minced garlic until just softened.

2 Using a sharp knife, coarsely chop the artichoke hearts. Add the artichoke pieces to the onion and garlic mixture in the pan. Pour in the hot vegetable bouillon, stirring.

3 Bring the mixture to a boil, then reduce the heat and let simmer, covered, for about 3 minutes.

4 Place the mixture in a food processor and blend until smooth. Alternatively, push the mixture through a strainer to remove any lumps.

5 Return the soup to the pan and stir in the light cream and fresh thyme.

6 Transfer the soup to a large bowl and cover, and then let chill in the refrigerator for about 3–4 hours.

7 Transfer the chilled soup to individual soup bowls and garnish with strips of sun-dried tomato. Serve with lots of fresh, crusty bread.

SERVES 4

1 tbsp olive oil
1 onion, chopped
1 garlic clove, minced
2 x 8 oz cans artichoke hearts, drained
2½ cups hot vegetable bouillon
²⁄₃ cup light cream
2 tbsp fresh thyme, stalks removed
2 sun-dried tomatoes, cut into strips
crusty bread to serve

NUTRITION
Calories 159; Sugars 2 g; Protein 2 g;
Carbohydrate 5 g; Fat 15 g; Saturates 6 g

easy

5 mins

15 mins

COOK'S TIP

Try adding 2 tablespoons of dry vermouth, such as Martini, to the soup in step 5, if you wish.

The Calabrian mountains in southern Italy provide large amounts of exotic mushrooms. They are rich in flavor and color and make a wonderful soup.

Calabrian Mushroom Soup

SERVES 4

2 tbsp olive oil
1 onion, chopped
1 lb/450 g mixed mushrooms, such as porcini, oyster, and white
1¼ cups milk
3¾ cups hot vegetable bouillon
8 slices of French baguette
3 tbsp butter, melted
2 garlic cloves, ground
¾ cup finely grated Gruyère cheese
salt and pepper

1 Heat the oil in a large skillet and cook the onion for 3–4 minutes, or until soft and golden.

2 Wipe each mushroom with a damp cloth and cut any large mushrooms into smaller, bite-size pieces.

3 Add the mushrooms to the skillet, stirring quickly to coat them in the oil.

4 Add the milk to the skillet, bring to a boil, cover and leave to simmer for about 5 minutes. Gradually stir in the hot vegetable bouillon.

5 Under a preheated broiler, toast the bread on both sides until golden.

6 Mix together the butter and garlic and then spoon generously over the toast.

7 Place the toast in the bottom of a large tureen or divide it among 4 individual serving bowls and pour over the hot soup. Top with the grated Gruyère cheese and serve at once.

NUTRITION
Calories *452*; Sugars *5 g*; Protein *15 g*; Carbohydrate *42 g*; Fat *26 g*; Saturates *12 g*

 easy
5 mins
20 mins

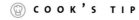 **COOK'S TIP**

Mushrooms absorb liquid, which can lessen the flavor and affect cooking properties. Wipe them with a damp cloth rather than rinsing them in water.

This fresh-tasting soup with dwarf beans, cucumber, and arugula can be served hot but is also good chilled on a hot summer's day.

Green Soup

1 Heat the oil in a large pan and sauté the onion and garlic for 3–4 minutes or until soft. Add the potato and cook for a further 2–3 minutes.

2 Stir in the bouillon, bring to a boil and leave to simmer for 5 minutes.

3 Add the cucumber to the pan and cook for a further 3 minutes or until the potatoes are tender. Test by inserting the tip of a knife into the potato cubes—it should pass through easily.

4 Add the arugula and allow to wilt. Then place the soup in a food processor and blend until smooth. Alternatively, before adding the arugula, mash the soup with a potato masher and push through a strainer, then chop the arugula finely and stir into the soup.

5 Bring a small pan of water to a boil and steam the beans for 3–4 minutes or until tender.

6 Add the beans to the soup, season and warm through.

SERVES 4

1 tbsp olive oil
1 onion, chopped
1 garlic clove, chopped
8 oz/225 g potato, peeled and cut into 1-inch/2.5-cm cubes
scant 3 cups vegetable or chicken bouillon
1 small cucumber or ½ large cucumber, cut into chunks
3 oz bunch arugula
¾ cup dwarf beans, trimmed and halved in length
salt and pepper

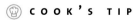 **COOK'S TIP**

Try using 1½ cups snow peas instead of the beans, if you prefer.

NUTRITION
Calories *121*; Sugars *2 g*; Protein *2 g*; Carbohydrate *10 g*; Fat *8 g*; Saturates *1 g*

⭐⭐ easy

5 mins

25–30 mins

The red kidney beans give
this soup a warm glow
as well as making it a
hearty dish.

Red Bean Soup

SERVES 4

scant 1 cup dried red kidney beans,
    soaked overnight
7½ cups water
1 large ham bone or bacon knuckle
2 carrots, chopped
1 large onion, chopped
2 celery stalks, thinly sliced
1 leek, trimmed, washed and sliced
1–2 bay leaves
2 tbsp olive oil
2–3 tomatoes, peeled and chopped
1 garlic clove, crushed
1 tbsp tomato paste
4½ tbsp arborio or risotto rice
1½ cups finely shredded green cabbage
salt and pepper

1 Drain the beans and place them in a pan with enough water to cover. Bring to a boil, then boil for 15 minutes to remove any harmful toxins. Reduce the heat and simmer for 45 minutes. Skim off any scum from the top.

2 Drain the beans and put into a clean pan with the water, ham bone or knuckle, carrots, onion, celery, leek, bay leaves, and olive oil. Bring to the boil, then cover and simmer for 1 hour or until the beans are very tender.

3 Discard the bay leaves and bone, reserving any ham pieces from the bone. Remove a small cupful of the beans and reserve. Purée or liquidize the soup in a food processor or blender, or push through a coarse strainer, and return to a clean pan.

4 Add the tomatoes, garlic, tomato paste, rice, and seasoning. Bring back to a boil and simmer for about 15 minutes or until the rice is tender.

5 Add the cabbage and reserved beans and ham, and continue to simmer for 5 minutes. Adjust the seasoning and serve very hot. If liked, a piece of toasted crusty bread may be put in the base of each soup bowl before ladling in the soup. If the soup is too thick, thin by adding a little boiling water or bouillon.

NUTRITION
Calories *184*; Sugars *5 g*; Protein *4 g*;
Carbohydrate *19 g*; Fat *11 g*; Saturates *2 g*

    easy

    8 hrs 10 mins

    2 hrs 40 mins

A thick vegetable soup which is a delicious meal in itself. Serve with Parmesan cheese and warm sun-dried tomato bread.

Garbanzo Bean Soup

1 Heat the oil in a large pan, add the leeks and zucchini and cook briskly for 5 minutes, stirring constantly.

2 Add the garlic, tomatoes, tomato paste, bay leaf, chicken bouillon, and garbanzo beans and stir to mix well.

3 Bring to a boil and simmer for 5 minutes.

4 Shred the spinach finely, add to the soup and cook for 2 minutes. Season.

5 Discard the bay leaf. Serve the soup immediately with freshly grated Parmesan cheese and warm sun-dried tomato bread.

SERVES 4

2 tbsp olive oil
2 leeks, sliced
2 zucchini, diced
2 garlic cloves, crushed
4 cups canned chopped tomatoes
1 tbsp tomato paste
1 fresh bay leaf
3¾ cups chicken bouillon
1½ cups canned garbanzo beans, drained and rinsed
8 oz/225 g spinach
salt and pepper

to serve
Parmesan cheese, freshly grated
sun-dried tomato bread

NUTRITION
Calories *297*; Sugars *0 g*; Protein *11 g*;
Carbohydrate *24 g*; Fat *18 g*; Saturates *2 g*

⭐   very easy
     5 mins
     15 mins

(👨‍🍳) COOK'S TIP

Garbanzo beans are used extensively in North African cuisine and are also found in Spanish, Middle Eastern and Indian cooking. They have a nutty flavor with a firm texture and are excellent canned.

Fresh pesto is a treat to the taste buds and very different in flavor from that available from supermarkets. Store fresh pesto in the refrigerator.

Potato *and* Pesto Soup

SERVES 4

3 strips rindless, smoked, fatty bacon finely chopped
1 lb/450 g floury potatoes finely chopped
1 lb/450 g onions finely chopped
2 tbsp olive oil
2 tbsp butter
2 ½ cups chicken bouillon
2 ½ cups milk
¾ cup dried conchigliette pasta shells
⅝ cup heavy cream
chopped fresh parsley
1 quantity Pesto Sauce (see page 133)
salt and pepper

to serve
Parmesan cheese shavings
garlic bread, toasted

1 Pan-fry the bacon in a large pan over a medium heat for 4 minutes. Add the olive oil, butter, potatoes, and onions and cook for 12 minutes, stirring constantly.

2 Add the bouillon and milk to the pan, bring to a boil and simmer for 10 minutes. Add the conchigliette and simmer for a further 10–12 minutes.

3 Blend in the cream and simmer for 5 minutes. Add the parsley, salt and pepper and 2 tablespoons of pesto sauce. Transfer the soup to serving bowls and serve with shavings of Parmesan cheese and toasted garlic bread.

NUTRITION
Calories *548*; Sugars *0 g*; Protein *11 g*;
Carbohydrate *10 g*; Fat *52 g*; Saturates *18 g*

easy

15 mins

50 mins

This quick and easy creamy soup has a lovely fresh tomato flavor.

Creamy Tomato Soup

1 Melt the butter in a large pan. Add the tomatoes and cook for 5 minutes until the skins start to wrinkle. Season to taste with salt and pepper.

2 Add the bouillon to the pan, bring to a boil, cover the pan, and simmer for 10 minutes.

3 Meanwhile, under a preheated broiler, lightly toast the ground almonds until golden-brown. This will take only 1–2 minutes, so watch them closely.

4 Remove the soup from the heat and place in a food processor and blend the mixture to form a smooth consistency. Alternatively, mash the soup with a potato masher.

5 Pass the soup through a strainer to remove any tomato skin or seeds.

6 Place the soup back in the pan and return to the heat. Stir in the milk or cream, ground almonds, and sugar. Warm the soup through and add the shredded basil just before serving.

7 Transfer the creamy tomato soup to warm soup bowls and serve hot.

SERVES 4

3 tbsp butter
1 ½ lb/674 g ripe tomatoes, preferably plum, roughly chopped
3¾ cups hot vegetable bouillon
⅔ cup milk or light cream
½ cup ground almonds
1 tsp sugar
2 tbsp shredded fresh basil leaves
salt and pepper

NUTRITION
Calories *218*; Sugars *10 g*; Protein *3 g*;
Carbohydrate *10 g*; Fat *19 g*; Saturates *11 g*

✪✪	easy
◔	5 mins
◕	25–30 mins

👨‍🍳 **COOK'S TIP**

Very fine bread crumbs can be used instead of the ground almonds, if you prefer. Toast them in the same way as the almonds and add with the milk or cream in step 6.

Plum tomatoes are ideal for making soups and sauces, as they have denser, less watery flesh than round varieties.

Tomato *and* Pasta Soup

SERVES 4

4 tbsp unsalted butter
1 large onion, chopped
2½ cups vegetable bouillon
2 lb/900 g Italian plum tomatoes, skinned and coarsely chopped
pinch of baking soda
2 cups dried fusilli
1 tbsp superfine sugar
⅝ cup heavy cream
salt and pepper
fresh basil leaves, to garnish
deep-fried croûtons, to serve

1 Melt the butter in a large pan, then add the onion and cook for 3 minutes. Add 1¼ cups of vegetable bouillon to the pan, with the tomatoes and baking soda. Bring the soup to a boil and simmer for 20 minutes.

2 Remove the pan from the heat and set aside to cool. When cool, purée the soup in a blender or food processor and pour through a fine strainer back into the pan.

3 Add the remaining vegetable bouillon and the fusilli to the pan, and season to taste with salt and pepper.

4 Add the sugar to the pan and bring to a boil, then lower the heat and simmer for about 15 minutes.

5 Pour the soup into a warm tureen. Swirl the heavy cream around the surface of the soup and garnish with fresh basil leaves. Serve immediately with the hot croûtons.

NUTRITION
Calories *503*; Sugars *16 g*; Protein 9 *g*;
Carbohydrate *59 g*; Fat *28 g*; Saturates *17 g*

⭐⭐ easy
🕐 5 mins
🕐 40 mins

  COOK'S TIP

To make orange and tomato soup, simply use half the quantity of vegetable bouillon, topped up with the same amount of fresh orange juice and garnish the soup with orange peel.

A minestra is a soup cooked with pasta; farfalline, a small bow-shaped variety, is used in this case. Served with lentils, this hearty soup is a meal in itself.

Brown Lentil Soup *with* Pasta

1 Place the bacon in a large skillet together with the onions, garlic, and celery. Dry-fry for 4–5 minutes, stirring, until the onion is tender and the bacon is just beginning to brown.

2 Add the farfalline or spaghetti pieces to the skillet and cook, stirring, for about 1 minute to coat the pasta well in the oil.

3 Add the lentils and the bouillon and bring to a boil. Reduce the heat and leave to simmer for 12–15 minutes or until the pasta is tender.

4 Remove the skillet from the heat and stir in the chopped fresh mint.

5 Transfer the soup to warm soup bowls and serve immediately.

SERVES 4

4 strips sliced bacon, cut into small squares
1 onion, chopped
2 garlic cloves, minced
2 celery stalks, chopped
¼ cup farfalline or spaghetti, broken into small pieces
14 oz canned brown lentils, drained
5 cups hot ham or vegetable bouillon
2 tbsp chopped, fresh mint

NUTRITION
Calories *225*; Sugars *1 g*; Protein *13 g*; Carbohydrate *27 g*; Fat *8 g*; Saturates *3 g*

 very easy
 5 mins
 25 mins

COOK'S TIP

If you prefer to use dried lentils, add the bouillon before the pasta and cook for 1–1¼ hours, until the lentils are tender. Add the pasta and cook for an additional 12–15 minutes.

Italian cooks have created some very heart-warming soups and this is the most famous of all.

Minestrone

SERVES 4

4 tbsp butter
¼ cup olive oil
½ cup finely diced rindless fatty bacon
3 garlic cloves, finely chopped
3 large onions, finely chopped
2 celery stalks, finely chopped
2 large carrots, finely chopped
2 large potatoes, finely chopped
½ cup dwarf beans, finely chopped
1 scant cup finely chopped zucchini
6⅞ cups vegetable or chicken bouillon
1 bunch fresh basil, finely chopped
½ cup chopped tomatoes
2 tbsp tomato paste
4 oz/100 g Parmesan cheese peel
3 oz/75 g dried spaghetti, broken up
salt and pepper
freshly grated Parmesan cheese, to serve

1 Heat the butter and oil together in a large pan, then add the bacon and cook for 2 minutes. Add the garlic and onion and cook for 2 minutes, then stir in the celery, carrots, and potatoes, and cook for an additional 2 minutes.

2 Add the beans to the pan and cook for 2 minutes. Stir in the zucchini and cook for an additional 2 minutes. Cover the pan and cook all the vegetables, stirring frequently, for 15 minutes.

3 Add the bouillon, basil, tomatoes, tomato paste, and Parmesan cheese peel and season to taste. Bring to a boil, then lower the heat and simmer for 1 hour. Remove and discard the cheese peel.

4 Add the spaghetti to the pan and cook for a further 20 minutes.

5 Serve in large, warm soup bowls sprinkled with generous amounts of freshly grated Parmesan cheese.

NUTRITION
Calories *231*; Sugars *3 g*; Protein *8 g*;
Carbohydrate *14 g*; Fat *16 g*; Saturates *7 g*

 easy
10 mins
1 hr 45 mins

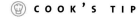

🍽 **COOK'S TIP**
You can use any variety of small pasta shape in place of the spaghetti.

A dish with proud Mediterranean origins, this soup is a winter warmer. Serve with warm, crusty bread and, if you like, a slice of cheese.

Bean *and* Pasta Soup

1 Put the soaked beans into a large pan, cover with cold water, and bring to a boil. Boil rapidly for 15 minutes to remove any harmful toxins. Drain the beans in a colander.

2 Heat the oil in a pan over a medium heat and pan-fry the onions until they are just beginning to change color. Stir in the garlic and cook for 1 further minute. Stir in the chopped tomatoes, oregano and the tomato paste and pour on the water. Add the beans, bring to a boil and cover the pan. Simmer for 45 minutes or until the beans are almost tender.

3 Add the pasta, season the soup with salt and pepper to taste, and stir in the sun-dried tomatoes. Return the soup to a boil, partly cover the pan and continue cooking for 10 minutes, or until the pasta is nearly tender.

4 Stir in the cilantro or parsley. Taste the soup and adjust the seasoning if necessary. Transfer to a warmed soup tureen to serve. Sprinkle with the cheese and serve hot.

SERVES 4

generous 1 cup dried navy beans, soaked overnight, drained and rinsed

4 tbsp olive oil

2 large onions, sliced

3 garlic cloves, chopped

2 cups canned chopped tomatoes

1 tsp dried oregano

1 tsp tomato paste

3½ cups water

generous 1 cup small pasta shapes, such as fusilli or conchigliette

4½ oz/125 g sun-dried tomatoes, drained and thinly sliced

1 tbsp chopped fresh cilantro, or flatleaf parsley

salt and pepper

2 tbsp freshly grated Parmesan cheese, to serve

NUTRITION
Calories *463*; Sugars *5 g*; Protein *13 g*; Carbohydrate *30 g*; Fat *33 g*; Saturates *7 g*

⭐⭐ easy

  8 hrs 10 mins

  1 hr 15 mins

This soup is the traditional *Minestra* served at Easter and Christmas in the province of Parma.

Ravioli *alla* Parmigiana

SERVES 4

10 oz/280 g Basic Pasta Dough (see page 9)
5 cups veal bouillon
freshly grated Parmesan cheese, to serve

filling
1 cup freshly grated Parmesan cheese
1²/₃ cup fine white bread crumbs
2 eggs
½ cup Espagnole Sauce (see page 15)
1 small onion, finely chopped
1 tsp freshly grated nutmeg

1 Make the Basic Pasta Dough. Carefully roll out 2 sheets of the pasta dough and cover with a damp dish towel while you make the filling for the ravioli.

2 To make the filling, mix together the Parmesan cheese, fine white bread crumbs, eggs, Espagnole Sauce, onion, and the freshly grated nutmeg in a large mixing bowl.

3 Place spoonfuls of the filling at regular intervals on the first sheet of pasta dough. Cover with the second sheet of pasta dough and cut into squares, then seal the edges by pressing them firmly together.

4 Bring the veal bouillon to a boil in a large pan. Add the ravioli to the pan and cook for about 15 minutes.

5 Transfer the soup and ravioli to warm serving bowls and serve at once, generously sprinkled with freshly grated Parmesan cheese.

NUTRITION
Calories 554; Sugars 3 g; Protein 26 g;
Carbohydrate 64 g; Fat 24 g; Saturates 9 g

challenging

4 hrs 30 mins–5 hrs

25 mins

This satisfying soup makes a good lunch or supper dish and you can use any vegetables that you have at hand. Children will love the tiny pasta shapes.

Chicken *and* Pasta Soup

1 Heat the oil in a large pan and quickly sauté the chicken and vegetables until they are lightly colored.

2 Stir in the bouillon and herbs. Bring to a boil and add the pasta shapes. Return to a boil, then cover and simmer for 10 minutes, stirring occasionally to prevent the pasta shapes sticking together.

3 Season with salt and pepper to taste and sprinkle with Parmesan cheese, if using. Serve with fresh crusty bread.

SERVES 4

12 oz/250 g boneless chicken breasts, finely diced
2 tbsp sunflower oil
1 medium onion, diced
1½ cups diced carrots
2 cups cauliflower flowerets
3¾ cups chicken bouillon
2 tsp dried mixed herbs
1½ cups small pasta shapes
salt and pepper

to serve
Parmesan cheese (optional)
crusty bread

NUTRITION
Calories *185*; Sugars *5 g*; Protein *17 g*;
Carbohydrate *20 g*; Fat *5 g*; Saturates *1 g*

easy
5 mins
15–20 mins

 COOK'S TIP

You can use any small pasta shapes for this soup—try conchigliette, ditalini, or even spaghetti broken up into small pieces. For a fun soup for children, you could add animal-shaped or alphabet pasta.

Veal plays an important role in Italian cuisine and there are dozens of recipes for all cuts of this meat.

Tuscan Veal Broth

SERVES 4

⅓ cup dried peas, soaked for 2 hours, and drained
2 lb/900 g boned neck of veal, diced
5 cups beef or brown bouillon (see page 16)
2⅓ cups water
⅓ cup barley, washed
1 large carrot, diced
1 small turnip (about 6 oz/175 g), diced
1 large leek, thinly sliced
1 red onion, finely chopped
½ cup chopped tomatoes
1 fresh basil sprig
¾ cup dried vermicelli
salt and white pepper

1 Put the peas, veal, bouillon, and water into a large pan and bring to a boil over a low heat. Using a draining spoon, skim off any scum that rises to the surface of the liquid.

2 When all of the scum has been removed, add the barley and a pinch of salt to the mixture. Simmer gently over a low heat for 25 minutes.

3 Add the carrot, turnip, leek, onion, tomatoes, and basil to the pan, and season with salt and pepper to taste. Let simmer for about 2 hours, skimming the surface, using a draining spoon, from time to time. Remove the pan from the heat and set aside for 2 hours.

4 Set the pan over a medium heat and bring to a boil. Add the vermicelli and cook for 12 minutes. Season with salt and pepper to taste, and remove and discard the basil. Ladle into soup bowls and serve immediately.

NUTRITION

Calories *420*; Sugars *5 g*; Protein *54 g*;
Carbohydrate *37 g*; Fat *7 g*; Saturates *2 g*

 challenging
4 hrs 15 mins
2 hrs 45 mins

🍳 COOK'S TIP

Lentils or split peas would work equally well in this recipe. These would not need to be soaked, reducing the preparation time.

There are many varieties of fish soup in Italy, some including shellfish. This one, from Tuscany, is more like a chowder.

Fish Soup

1 Cut the fish into slices and put into a pan with half the onion and celery, the parsley sprigs, bay leaves, wine, and water. Bring to a boil, cover and simmer for 25 minutes.

2 Strain the fish bouillon and discard the vegetables. Skin the fish, remove any bones and reserve the fish.

3 Heat the oil in a pan. Cook the remaining onion and celery with the garlic and carrot, until soft, but not colored, stirring occasionally. Add the tomatoes, potatoes, tomato paste, oregano, reserved bouillon and seasoning. Bring to a boil and simmer for about 15 minutes or until the potato is almost tender.

4 Meanwhile, thoroughly scrub the mussels. Add the mussels to the pan with the shrimp and leave to simmer for about 5 minutes or until the mussels have opened (discard any that remain closed).

5 Return the reserved fish to the soup with the chopped parsley, bring back to the boil and simmer for 5 minutes. Adjust the seasoning.

6 Serve the soup in warmed bowls with chunks of fresh crusty bread, or put a toasted slice of crusty bread in the bottom of each bowl before adding the soup. If possible, remove a few half shells from the mussels before serving.

SERVES 4

2 lb 4 oz/1 kg assorted prepared fish (including mixed fish fillets, squid, etc.)
2 onions, thinly sliced
2 celery stalks, thinly sliced
fresh sprigs of parsley
2 bay leaves
²/₃ cup white wine
4 cups water
2 tbsp olive oil
1 garlic clove, crushed
1 carrot, finely chopped
2 cups canned peeled tomatoes, puréed
2 potatoes, chopped
1 tbsp tomato paste
½ tsp dried oregano
12 oz/350 g fresh mussels
6 oz/175 g peeled shrimp
2 tbsp chopped fresh parsley
salt and pepper
crusty bread, to serve

NUTRITION
Calories 305; Sugars 3 g; Protein 47 g; Carbohydrate 11 g; Fat 7 g; Saturates 1 g

★★★   moderate
    5–10 mins
   1 hr

Snacks *and* Appetizers

Appetizers are known as *antipasti* in Italy which is translated as meaning "before the main course." Antipasti usually come in three categories: meat, fish, and vegetables. There are many varieties of cold meats, including ham, invariably sliced paper-thin. All varieties of fish are popular in Italy, including squid (calamari), octopus, and cuttlefish. Seafood is also highly prized, especially huge shrimp, mussels and fresh sardines. Numerous vegetables feature in Italian cuisine and are an important part of the daily diet. They are served as an appetizer, as an accompaniment to main dishes, or as a course on their own. In Italy, vegetables are cooked only until *al dente* and still slightly crisp. This ensures that they retain more nutrients and the colors of the vegetables remain bright and appealing.

Nudo or naked is the word used to describe this mixture, which can also be made into thin crêpes or used as a filling for tortelloni.

Spinach *and* Ricotta Patties

SERVES 4

1 lb/450 g fresh spinach
8 oz ricotta cheese
1 egg, beaten
2 tsp fennel seeds, lightly ground
½ cup finely grated romano
  or Parmesan cheese
1 oz/25 g all-purpose flour, mixed with 1 tsp
  dried thyme
5 tbsp butter
2 garlic cloves, minced
salt and pepper

1 Wash the spinach and trim off any long stalks. Place in a pan and cover, then cook for 4–5 minutes, or until wilted. This will probably have to be done in batches as the volume of spinach is quite large. Place in a colander and let drain and cool.

2 Mash the ricotta and beat in the egg and the fennel seeds. Season with plenty of salt and pepper, then stir in the romano or Parmesan cheese.

3 Squeeze as much excess water as possible from the spinach, then finely chop the leaves. Stir into the cheese mixture.

4 Taking about 1 tablespoon of the spinach and cheese mixture, shape it into a ball, then flatten it slightly to form a patty. Gently roll in the seasoned flour. Continue this process until all of the mixture has been used up.

5 Half fill a large skillet with water and bring to a boil. Carefully add the patties and cook for 3–4 minutes, or until they rise to the surface. Remove with a draining spoon.

6 Melt the butter in a pan. Add the garlic and cook for 2–3 minutes. Pour the garlic butter over the patties and season with pepper, then serve at once.

NUTRITION
Calories *374*; Sugars *4 g*; Protein *16 g*;
Carbohydrate *9 g*; Fat *31 g*; Saturates *19 g*

  moderate

5 mins

30 mins

Colorful marinated Mediterranean vegetables make a tasty starter. Serve with fresh bread or Tomato Toasts (see below).

Pepper Salad

1 Heat the oil in a large, heavy-based skillet. Add the onion, bell peppers, zucchini, and garlic and pan-fry gently for 20 minutes, stirring occasionally.

2 Add the vinegar, anchovies, olives, and seasoning to taste, mix thoroughly and leave to cool.

3 Spoon the salad on to individual plates and sprinkle with the basil.

4 To make the tomato toasts, cut the French baguette diagonally into ½-inch/1-cm slices.

5 Mix the garlic, tomato, oil, and seasoning together, and spread thinly over each slice of bread.

6 Place the bread on a cookie sheet, drizzle with the olive oil and bake in a preheated oven, 425°F/220°C, for 5–10 minutes, until crisp. Serve the tomato toasts with the Pepper Salad.

SERVES 4

3 tbsp olive oil
1 onion, cut into wedges
2 red bell peppers, halved, deseeded and thickly sliced
2 yellow bell peppers, halved, deseeded and thickly sliced
2 large zucchini, sliced
2 garlic cloves, sliced
1 tbsp balsamic vinegar
1¾ oz/50 g anchovy fillets, chopped
¼ cup black olives, halved and pitted
1 tbsp chopped fresh basil
salt and pepper

tomato toasts
1 small French baguette
1 garlic clove, crushed
1 tomato, peeled and chopped
2 tbsp olive oil

NUTRITION
Calories *234*; Sugars *4 g*; Protein *6 g*;
Carbohydrate *15 g*; Fat *17 g*; Saturates *2 g*

✪✪✪   moderate
     5-10 mins
🕐   35 mins

Thin slices of eggplant are pan-fried in olive oil and garlic, and then topped with pesto sauce and finely grated mozzarella cheese.

Eggplant Rolls

SERVES 4

2 eggplants, thinly sliced lengthwise
5 tbsp olive oil, plus extra for brushing
1 garlic clove, crushed
4 tbsp Pesto Sauce (see page 133)
1½ cups grated mozzarella cheese
fresh basil leaves, torn into pieces
salt and pepper
fresh basil leaves, to garnish

1 Place the eggplant slices in a colander or on a plate and sprinkle liberally with salt. Set aside for 10–15 minutes to extract the bitter juices. Turn the slices over and repeat. Rinse thoroughly under cold running water and drain on paper towels.

2 Heat the olive oil in a large skillet and add the garlic. Add the eggplant slices, a few at a time, and pan-fry lightly on both sides over medium heat. Drain them on paper towels.

3 Spread the pesto on one side of the eggplant slices. Top with the grated mozzarella and sprinkle with the torn basil leaves. Season to taste with salt and pepper. Roll up the slices and secure with wooden toothpicks.

4 Lightly brush an ovenproof dish with a little olive oil and arrange the eggplant rolls in it. Place in a preheated oven, 350°F/180°C, and bake for 8–10 minutes.

5 Transfer the eggplant rolls to a warmed serving plate. Sprinkle with fresh basil leaves and serve immediately.

NUTRITION
Calories *278*; Sugars *2 g*; Protein *4 g*;
Carbohydrate *2 g*; Fat *28 g*; Saturates *7 g*

★★★ moderate
◔ 15–20 mins
🕐 20 mins

 COOK'S TIP

You could use zucchini instead of the eggplant for a change. They will take less time to fry.

These are delicious as an appetizer or light supper dish. You can vary the filling with another fish if you prefer.

Pancakes *with* Smoked Fish

1 To make the pancake batter, strain the flour and salt into a large bowl and make a well in the center. Add the egg and, using a wooden spoon, begin to draw in the flour. Slowly add the milk and beat together to form a smooth batter. Set aside until required.

2 Place the fish in a large skillet, add the milk and bring to a boil. Simmer for 10 minutes or until the fish begins to flake. Drain thoroughly, reserving the milk and the fish.

3 Melt the butter in a saucepan. Add the flour, mix to a paste and cook for 2–3 minutes. Remove the pan from the heat and add the reserved milk a little at a time, stirring to make a smooth sauce. Repeat with the fish bouillon. Return to the heat and bring to a boil, stirring. Stir in the Parmesan and season with salt and pepper to taste.

4 Grease a skillet with oil. Add 2 tablespoons of the pancake batter, swirling it around the pan and cook for 2–3 minutes. Loosen the sides with a spatula and flip over the pancake. Cook for 2–3 minutes until golden; repeat. Stack the pancakes with sheets of baking parchment between them and keep warm in the oven.

5 Stir the flaked fish, peas, and shrimp into half of the sauce and use to fill each pancake. Pour over the remaining sauce, top with the Gruyère cheese, and bake for 20 minutes, until golden.

SERVES 4

pancakes
scant 1 cup all purpose flour
½ tsp salt
1 egg, beaten
¼ cup milk
1 tbsp oil, for pan-frying

sauce
1 lb/450 g smoked haddock, skinned
1¼ cups milk
3 tbsp butter or margarine
⅓ cup flour
¼ cups fish bouillon
¾ cup grated Parmesan cheese
¾ cup frozen peas, thawed
4 oz/100 g shrimp, cooked and peeled
½ cup Gruyère cheese, grated
salt and pepper

NUTRITION
Calories *399*; Sugars *6 g*; Protein *36 g*; Carbohydrate *25 g*; Fat *18 g*; Saturates *10 g*

⭐⭐⭐   moderate

🕐   15 mins

    40–45 mins

These deep-fried mozzarella sandwiches are a tasty snack at any time of the day, or serve smaller triangles as an antipasto with drinks.

Mozzarella *in* Carriages

SERVES 4

8 slices bread, preferably slightly stale, crusts removed
4 oz/100 g mozzarella cheese, sliced thickly
⅓ cup chopped black olives
8 canned anchovy fillets, drained and chopped
16 fresh basil leaves
4 eggs, beaten
⅔ cup milk
oil, for deep-frying
salt and pepper

1 Cut each slice of bread into 2 triangles. Top 8 of the bread triangles with equal amounts of the mozzarella slices, olives, and chopped anchovies.

2 Place the basil leaves on top and season with salt and pepper to taste.

3 Lay the other 8 triangles of bread over the top and press down round the edges to seal.

4 Mix the eggs and milk together and pour into an ovenproof dish. Add the sandwiches and leave to soak for about 5 minutes.

5 Heat the oil in a large saucepan to 350°–375°F/180°–190°C or until a cube of bread browns in 30 seconds.

6 Before cooking the sandwiches, squeeze the edges together again.

7 Carefully place the sandwiches in the oil and deep-fry for 2 minutes or until golden, turning once. Remove the sandwiches with a draining spoon and drain on paper towels. You will have to cook the sandwiches in batches. Serve immediately while still hot.

NUTRITION
Calories *379*; Sugars *22 g*; Protein *20 g*; Carbohydrate *28 g*; Fat *22 g*; Saturates *5 g*

 COOK'S TIP

Using bread about 1 to 2 days old is much easier to handle and is much less likely to crumble.

⭐ very easy

🕐 20 mins

🕐 5–10 mins

Fennel is a very versatile vegetable, which is good cooked or used raw in salads. It is an especially popular ingredient in many Italian dishes.

Baked Fennel

1 Using a sharp knife, trim the fennel, discarding any tough outer leaves, and cut the bulb into fourths.

2 Bring a large pan of water to a boil, add the fennel and celery, and cook for 8–10 minutes or until just tender. Remove with a draining spoon and drain.

3 Place the fennel, celery, and sun-dried tomatoes in a large ovenproof dish.

4 Mix the crushed tomatoes and oregano together, and pour the mixture over the fennel.

5 Sprinkle the surface evenly with the Parmesan cheese and bake in a preheated oven, 375°F/190°C, for 20 minutes or until hot. Serve as a starter with fresh crusty bread or as a vegetable side dish.

SERVES 4

2 fennel bulbs
2 celery stalks, cut into 3-inch/7.5-cm pieces
6 sun-dried tomatoes, halved
scant 1 cup crushed tomatoes
2 tsp dried oregano
²/₃ cup freshly grated Parmesan cheese

NUTRITION
Calories 111; Sugars 6 g; Protein 7 g;
Carbohydrate 7 g; Fat 7 g; Saturates 3 g

easy

 10 mins

 35 mins

This quick and easy casserole can be eaten as a healthy supper dish or as a side dish to accompany sausages or grilled fish.

Casserole *of* Beans *in* Tomato Sauce

SERVES 4

14 oz/400 g canned cannellini beans
14 oz/400 g canned borlotti beans
2 tbsp olive oil
1 celery stalk, chopped
2 garlic cloves, chopped
6 oz baby onions, halved
1 lb/450 g tomatoes
3 oz/75 g arugula

1 Drain both cans of beans and reserve 6 tablespoons of the liquid.

2 Heat the oil in a large pan. Add the celery, garlic, and onions and sauté for 5 minutes, or until the onions are golden.

3 Cut a cross in the base of each tomato and plunge them into a bowl of boiling water for 30 seconds until the skins split. Remove them with a draining spoon and let stand until cool enough to handle. Peel off the skin and chop the flesh. Add the tomato flesh and the reserved bean liquid to the pan and cook for 5 minutes.

4 Add the beans to the pan and cook for an additional 3–4 minutes, or until the beans are hot.

5 Stir in the arugula and allow to wilt slightly before serving.

NUTRITION
Calories *273*; Sugars *8 g*; Protein *15 g*;
Carbohydrate *40 g*; Fat *7 g*; Saturates *1 g*

⭐⭐⭐   moderate
🕐   10 mins
🕐   15 mins

 COOK'S TIP

You could use spinach in place of the arugula if unavailable.

This dish makes an
excellent appetizer, or is
great served as a snack at
a drinks party.

Crostini *alla* Fiorentina

1 Heat the oil in a pan, add the onion, celery, carrot, and garlic, and cook gently
for 4–5 minutes or until the onion is soft, but not colored.

2 Meanwhile, rinse and dry the chicken livers. Dry the calf's liver, and slice into
strips. Add the liver to the pan and pan-fry gently for a few minutes until the
strips are well sealed on all sides.

3 Add half of the wine and cook until it has mostly evaporated. Then add the
remaining wine, tomato paste, half of the parsley, the anchovy fillets,
bouillon, a little salt, and plenty of pepper.

4 Cover the pan and leave to simmer, stirring occasionally, for 15–20 minutes
or until tender and most of the liquid has been absorbed.

5 Leave the mixture to cool a little, then either coarsely mince or put into a
food processor and process to a chunky purée.

6 Return to the pan and add the butter, capers, and remaining parsley. Heat
through gently until the butter melts. Adjust the seasoning and turn out
into a bowl. Serve warm or cold spread on the slices of crusty bread and
sprinkled with chopped parsley.

SERVES 4

3 tbsp olive oil
1 onion, chopped
1 celery stalk, chopped
1 carrot, chopped
1–2 garlic cloves, crushed
4¹⁄₂ oz/125 g chicken livers
4¹⁄₂ oz/125 g calf's, lamb's or pig's liver
²⁄₃ cup red wine
1 tbsp tomato paste
2 tbsp chopped fresh parsley
3–4 canned anchovy fillets, finely chopped
2 tbsp bouillon or water
2–3 tbsp butter
1 tbsp capers
salt and pepper
small pieces of fried crusty bread, to serve
chopped fresh parsley, to garnish

NUTRITION
Calories 393; Sugars 2 g; Protein 17 g;
Carbohydrate 19 g; Fat 25 g; Saturates 9 g

✪✪✪   moderate
🕐   10 mins
🕐   40–45 mins

Deep-fried seafood is popular all around the Mediterranean, where fish of all kinds is fresh and abundant. Serve with garlic mayonnaise and lemon wedges.

Crispy Golden Seafood

SERVES 4

8 oz/225 g prepared squid
8 oz/225 g raw jumbo shrimp, peeled
5½ oz/150 g whitebait
oil, for deep-frying
⅓ cup all-purpose flour
1 tsp dried basil
salt and pepper

to serve
garlic mayonnaise (see Cook's Tip)
lemon wedges

1 Carefully rinse the squid, shrimp, and whitebait under cold running water, completely removing any dirt or grit.

2 Using a sharp knife, slice the squid into thin rings, but leaving the tentacles whole.

3 Heat the oil in a large saucepan to 350°–375°F/180–190°C or until a cube of bread browns in 30 seconds.

4 Place the flour in a bowl and season with the salt, pepper, and basil.

5 Roll the squid, shrimp, and whitebait in the seasoned flour until coated all over. Carefully shake off any excess flour.

6 Cook the seafood in the heated oil in batches for 2–3 minutes, or until crispy and golden all over. Remove all of the seafood with a draining spoon and let drain thoroughly on paper towels.

7 Transfer the deep-fried seafood to serving plates and serve with garlic mayonnaise and lemon wedges.

NUTRITION
Calories *393*; Sugars *0.2 g*; Protein *27 g*;
Carbohydrate *12 g*; Fat *26 g*; Saturates *3 g*

 easy

🕐 5 mins

🕐 15 mins

🍳 **COOK'S TIP**

To make garlic mayonnaise for serving with the deep-fried seafood, crush 2 garlic cloves, stir into 8 tablespoons of mayonnaise, then season with salt and pepper and a little chopped fresh parsley.

Simple to make, this spicy dish has Spanish chorizo sausage and anchovies as its main ingredients, and will set the taste buds tingling.

Chorizo *and* Wild Mushrooms

1 Bring a large pan of lightly salted water to a boil. Add the vermicelli and 1 tablespoon of the oil, and cook until just tender, but still firm to the bite. Drain, place on a large, warm serving plate, and keep warm.

2 Meanwhile heat the remaining oil in a large skillet. Add the garlic and cook for 1 minute. Add the chorizo and wild mushrooms and cook for 4 minutes, then add the red chiles and cook for another minute, until the mushrooms are just cooked through.

3 Pour the chorizo and wild mushroom mixture over the vermicelli and season with a little salt and pepper. Sprinkle over freshly grated Parmesan cheese, garnish with a lattice of anchovy fillets and serve immediately.

SERVES 4

1½ lb/675 g dried vermicelli
½ cup olive oil
2 garlic cloves, chopped finely
4½ oz/125 g chorizo, sliced
8 oz/225 g wild mushrooms
3 fresh red chiles, chopped
2 tbsp freshly grated Parmesan cheese
salt and pepper
10 anchovy fillets, to garnish

NUTRITION
Calories 495; Sugars 1 g; Protein 15 g; Carbohydrate 33 g; Fat 35 g; Saturates 5 g

⭐⭐ easy
🕐 5 mins
🕐 20 mins

🍴 **COOK'S TIP**

Always obtain wild mushrooms from a reliable source and never pick them yourself unless you are absolutely certain of their identity.

Served with fresh
Italian bread or tossed
with pesto, this makes a
mouthwatering light lunch.

Smoked Ham Linguine

SERVES 4

1 lb/450 g dried linguine
1 lb/450 g green broccoli flowerets
8 oz/225 g Italian smoked ham
⅝ cup Cheese Sauce (see page 15)
salt and pepper
Italian bread, to serve

1 Bring a large pan of lightly salted water to a boil. Add the linguine and broccoli flowerets and cook for 10 minutes, or until the linguine are tender, but still firm to the bite.

2 Drain the linguine and broccoli thoroughly, then set aside and keep warm.

3 Meanwhile, make the Cheese Sauce.

4 Cut the Italian smoked ham into thin strips. Toss the linguine, broccoli, and ham into the Italian Cheese Sauce and gently warm through over a low heat.

5 Transfer the pasta mixture to a warm serving dish. Sprinkle with black pepper and serve with Italian bread.

NUTRITION
Calories 537; Sugars 4 g; Protein 22 g;
Carbohydrate 71 g; Fat 29 g; Saturates 8 g

 moderate
25 mins
15 mins

🍳 **COOK'S TIP**

There are many types of Italian bread which would be suitable to serve with this dish. Ciabatta is made with olive oil and is available plain and with different ingredients, such as olives or sun-dried tomatoes.

Prepare the marinated eggplants well in advance so—when you are ready to eat—all you have to do is cook the pasta.

Eggplant *on a* Bed *of* Linguine

1 Put the vegetable bouillon, wine vinegar, and balsamic vinegar into a pan and bring to a boil over low heat. Add 2 teaspoons of the olive oil and the sprig of oregano and simmer gently for about 1 minute.

2 Add the eggplant slices to the pan, remove from the heat, and set aside for 10 minutes.

3 Meanwhile, make the marinade. Combine the oil, garlic, fresh oregano, almonds, red bell pepper, lime juice, orange rind and juice in a large bowl and season to taste with salt and pepper.

4 Carefully remove the eggplant slices from the pan with a draining spoon, and drain well. Add the eggplant slices to the marinade, mixing well to coat. Cover with plastic wrap and set aside in the refrigerator for about 12 hours.

5 Bring a large pan of lightly salted water to a boil. Add half of the remaining oil and the linguine. Bring back to a boil and cook for 8–10 minutes, until just tender, but still firm to the bite.

6 Drain the pasta thoroughly and toss with the remaining oil while it is still warm. Arrange the pasta on a serving plate with the eggplant slices and the marinade and serve immediately.

SERVES 4

²⁄₃ cup vegetable bouillon
²⁄₃ cup white wine vinegar
2 tsp balsamic vinegar
3 tbsp olive oil
fresh oregano sprig
1 lb/450 g eggplants, peeled and thinly sliced
14 oz/400 g dried linguine

marinade
2 tbsp extra-virgin olive oil
2 garlic cloves, crushed
2 tbsp chopped fresh oregano
2 tbsp finely chopped roasted almonds
2 tbsp diced red bell pepper
2 tbsp lime juice
grated rind and juice of 1 orange
salt and pepper

NUTRITION
Calories *378*; Sugars *3 g*; Protein *12 g*;
Carbohydrate *16 g*; Fat *30 g*; Saturates *3 g*

★★★★ challenging
        12 hrs 15 mins
        15 mins

This is a classic combination in which the smooth, creamy cheese balances the sharper taste of the spinach.

Spinach *and* Ricotta Shells

SERVES 4

400 g/14 oz dried lumache rigate grande
5 tbsp olive oil
1 cup fresh white bread crumbs
½ cup milk
10 oz/225 g frozen spinach, thawed and drained
8 oz/225g ricotta cheese
pinch of freshly grated nutmeg
2 cups canned chopped tomatoes, drained
1 garlic clove, crushed
salt and pepper

1 Bring a large pan of lightly salted water to a boil. Add the lumache and 1 tablespoon of the olive oil and cook for 8–10 minutes, until just tender, but still firm to the bite. Drain the pasta, refresh under cold water and set aside until required.

2 Put the bread crumbs, milk, and 3 tablespoons of the remaining olive oil in a food processor and work to combine.

3 Add the spinach and ricotta cheese to the food processor and work to a smooth mixture. Transfer to a bowl, stir in the nutmeg, and season with salt and pepper to taste.

4 Mix together the tomatoes, garlic, and remaining oil, and spoon the mixture into the base of a large ovenproof dish.

5 Using a teaspoon, fill the lumache with the spinach and ricotta mixture and arrange on top of the tomato mixture in the dish. Cover and bake in a preheated oven at 350°F/180°C, for 20 minutes. Serve hot.

NUTRITION
Calories *673*; Sugars *10 g*; Protein *23 g*; Carbohydrate *93 g*; Fat *26 g*; Saturates *8 g*

moderate
10 mins
30 mins

🍳 **COOK'S TIP**

Ricotta is a creamy Italian cheese traditionally made from ewe's milk whey. It is soft and white, with a smooth texture and a slightly sweet flavor. It should be used within 2–3 days of purchase.

This colorful light meal can be made with a variety of different pasta, including spaghetti and linguine.

Fettuccine *with* Anchovy *and* Spinach

1 Trim off any tough spinach stalks. Rinse the spinach leaves and place them in a large pan with only the water that is clinging to them after washing. Cover and cook over a high heat, shaking the pan from time, until the spinach has wilted, but retains its color. Drain well, set aside, and keep warm.

2 Bring a large pan of lightly salted water to a boil. Add the fettuccine, bring back to a boil, and cook for 8–10 minutes until it is just tender, but still firm to the bite.

3 Meanwhile, heat 4 tablespoons of the olive oil in a pan. Add the pinenuts and fry until golden. Remove the pinenuts from the pan with a draining spoon and set aside until required.

4 Add the garlic to the pan and pan-fry until golden. Add the anchovies and stir in the spinach. Cook, stirring constantly, for 2–3 minutes until heated through. Return the pinenuts to the pan.

5 Drain the fettuccine, toss in the remaining olive oil, and transfer to a warm serving dish. Spoon the anchovy and spinach sauce over the fettuccine, toss lightly, and serve immediately.

SERVES 4

2 lb/900 g fresh young spinach leaves
14 oz/400 g dried fettuccine
5 tbsp olive oil
3 tbsp pinenuts
3 garlic cloves, crushed
8 canned anchovy fillets, drained and chopped
salt

NUTRITION
Calories *619*; Sugars *5 g*; Protein *21 g*; Carbohydrate *67 g*; Fat *31 g*; Saturates *3 g*

⊗⊗   easy
◔   10 mins
⏱   25 mins

 COOK'S TIP

If you are in a hurry, you can use frozen spinach. Thaw and drain it thoroughly, pressing out as much moisture as possible. Cut the leaves into strips and add to the dish with the anchovies in step 4.

This simple, creamy
pasta sauce is a true classic
Italian recipe.

Tagliarini *with* Gorgonzola

SERVES 4

2 tbsp butter
2 cups Gorgonzola cheese, roughly crumbled
⅝ cup heavy cream
2 tbsp dry white wine
1 tsp cornstarch
4 fresh sage sprigs, finely chopped
14 oz/400 g dried tagliarini
2 tbsp olive oil
salt and white pepper

1 Melt the butter in a heavy-bottomed pan. Stir in 1½ cups of the Gorgonzola cheese and melt, over a low heat, for about 2 minutes.

2 Add the cream, wine, and cornstarch and beat with a whisk until fully incorporated.

3 Stir in the sage and season to taste with salt and white pepper. Bring to a boil over a low heat, whisking constantly, until the sauce thickens. Remove from the heat and set aside while you cook the pasta.

4 Bring a large pan of lightly salted water to a boil. Add the tagliarini and 1 tablespoon of the olive oil. Cook the pasta for 12–14 minutes, or until just tender, then drain thoroughly and toss in the remaining olive oil. Transfer the pasta to a serving dish and keep warm.

5 Return the pan containing the sauce to a low heat to reheat the sauce, whisking constantly. Spoon the Gorgonzola sauce over the tagliarini, then generously sprinkle over the remaining cheese, and serve immediately.

NUTRITION
Calories *904*; Sugars *4 g*; Protein *27 g*;
Carbohydrate *83 g*; Fat *53 g*; Saturates *36 g*

easy

5 mins

20 mins

 COOK'S TIP

Gorgonzola is one of the world's oldest veined cheeses. When buying, check that it is creamy yellow with delicate green veining. Avoid hard or discolored cheese. It should have a rich, piquant aroma, not a bitter smell.

This light pasta dish has a delicate flavor ideally suited to a summer lunch.

Spaghetti *with* Ricotta Cheese

1 Bring a large pan of lightly salted water to a boil. Add the spaghetti and 1 tablespoon of the oil and cook until tender, but still firm to the bite.

2 Drain the pasta, return to the pan, and toss with the butter and chopped parsley. Set aside and keep warm.

3 To make the sauce, mix together the ground almonds, ricotta cheese, nutmeg, cinnamon, and unsweetened yogurt over a low heat to form a thick paste. Gradually stir in the remaining oil. When the oil has been fully incorporated, gradually stir in the hot chicken bouillon, until smooth. Season to taste.

4 Transfer the spaghetti to a warm serving dish, pour over the sauce and toss together well (see Cook's Tip, below). Sprinkle over the pinenuts, garnish with the flatleaf parsley, and serve warm.

SERVES 4

12 oz dried spaghetti
3 tbsp olive oil
3 tbsp butter
2 tbsp chopped fresh flatleaf parsley
1 cup freshly ground almonds
½ cup ricotta cheese
pinch of grated nutmeg
pinch of powdered cinnamon
⅝ cup unsweetened yogurt
4 fl oz/125ml hot chicken bouillon
1 tbsp pinenuts
salt and pepper
fresh flatleaf parsley sprigs, to garnish

NUTRITION
Calories 701; Sugars 12 g; Protein 17 g; Carbohydrate 73 g; Fat 40 g; Saturates 15 g

⭐⭐   easy
🕐   5 mins
🕐   25 mins

 COOK'S TIP

Use two large forks to toss spaghetti or other long pasta, so that it is thoroughly coated with the sauce. Special spaghetti forks are available from some cookware departments and kitchen stores.

This is quick and simple, but one of the nicest of Italian pan-fried fish dishes, served with penne.

Penne *with* Fried Mussels

SERVES 4

3½ cups dried penne
½ cup olive oil
1 lb/450 g mussels, cooked and shelled
1 tsp sea salt
⅔ cup flour
3½ oz/100 g sun-dried tomatoes, sliced
2 tbsp chopped fresh basil leaves
salt and pepper
1 lemon, sliced thinly, to garnish

1 Bring a large pan of lightly salted water to a boil. Add the penne and 1 tablespoon of the olive oil and cook for 8–10 minutes or until the pasta is just tender, but still firm to the bite.

2 Drain the pasta thoroughly and place in a large, warm serving dish. Set aside and keep warm while you cook the mussels.

3 Lightly sprinkle the mussels with the sea salt. Season the flour with salt and pepper to taste, sprinkle into a bowl and toss the mussels in the flour until well coated.

4 Heat the remaining oil in a large skillet. Add the mussels and pan-fry, stirring frequently, until a golden brown color.

5 Toss the mussels with the penne and sprinkle with the sun-dried tomatoes and basil leaves. Garnish with slices of lemon and serve immediately.

NUTRITION

Calories 537; Sugars 2 g; Protein 22 g;
Carbohydrate 62 g; Fat 24 g; Saturates 3 g

easy
10 mins
25 mins

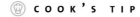 COOK'S TIP

Sun-dried tomatoes, used in Italy for a long time, have become popular elsewhere only quite recently. They are dried and then preserved in oil. They have a concentrated, roasted flavor and a dense texture.

Ribbed tubes of pasta are filled with tuna and ricotta cheese, and then baked in a creamy sauce.

Baked Tuna *and* Ricotta Rigatoni

1 Lightly grease a large ovenproof dish with butter.

2 Bring a large pan of lightly salted water to a boil. Add the rigatoni and olive oil and cook for 8–10 minutes, until just tender, but still firm to the bite. Drain the pasta and set aside until cool enough to handle.

3 Meanwhile, in a bowl, mix together the tuna and ricotta cheese to form a soft paste. Spoon the mixture into a pastry bag and use to fill the rigatoni. Arrange the filled pasta tubes side by side in the prepared ovenproof dish.

4 To make the sauce, mix the cream and Parmesan cheese, and season with salt and pepper to taste. Spoon the sauce over the rigatoni and top with the sun-dried tomatoes, arranged in a criss-cross pattern. Bake in a preheated oven, at 400°F/200°C, for 20 minutes. Serve hot straight from the dish.

SERVES 4

butter, for greasing
1 lb/450 g dried rigatoni
1 tbsp olive oil
7 oz/200 g canned flaked tuna, drained
8 oz/225 g ricotta cheese
½ cup heavy cream
2 ⅔ cups grated Parmesan cheese
4 oz/125 g sun-dried tomatoes, drained and sliced
salt and pepper

NUTRITION
Calories 949; Sugars 5 g; Protein 51 g; Carbohydrate 85 g; Fat 48 g; Saturates 26 g

moderate

15 mins

30 mins

COOK'S TIP

For a vegetarian alternative of this recipe, simply substitute a mixture of pitted and chopped black olives and chopped walnuts for the tuna. Follow exactly the same cooking method.

This filling vegetarian dish is perfect for an inexpensive and quick lunch.

Rotelle *with* Spicy Italian Sauce

SERVES 4

5 tbsp olive oil
3 garlic cloves, ground
2 fresh red chiles, chopped
1 fresh green chile, chopped
⅞ cup Italian Red Wine Sauce (see page 15)
3½ cups dried rotelle pasta
salt and pepper
warm Italian bread, to serve

1 Heat 4 tablespoons of the oil in a pan. Add the garlic and chiles and cook for 3 minutes.

2 Stir in the Italian Red Wine Sauce and season with salt and pepper to taste. Simmer gently over a low heat for 20 minutes.

3 Bring a large pan of lightly salted water to a boil. Add the rotelle and the remaining oil and cook for 8 minutes, or until just tender, but still firm to the bite. Drain the pasta.

4 Toss the rotelle in the spicy sauce, then transfer to a warm serving dish. Serve with warm Italian bread.

NUTRITION

Calories 530; Sugars 4 g; Protein 13 g;
Carbohydrate 78 g; Fat 18 g; Saturates 3 g

 moderate

10 mins

1 hr

 COOK'S TIP

Take care when using fresh chiles. Handle them as little as possible—wear rubber gloves if necessary. Always wash your hands thoroughly afterward and don't touch your face or eyes before you have washed your hands.

Deliciously sweet roasted tomatoes are filled with home-made lemon mayonnaise and tuna.

Tuna-Stuffed Tomatoes

1 Halve the tomatoes and scoop out the seeds. Divide the sun-dried tomato paste among the tomato halves and spread around the inside of the skin.

2 Place on a cookie sheet and roast in a preheated oven at 400°F/200°C for 12–15 minutes. Leave to cool slightly.

3 Meanwhile, make the mayonnaise. In a food processor, blend the egg yolks and lemon juice with the lemon rind, until smooth. Once mixed and with the motor still running slowly, add the olive oil. Stop the processor as soon as the mayonnaise has thickened. Alternatively, use a hand whisk, beating the mixture continuously until it thickens.

4 Add the tuna and capers to the mayonnaise and season.

5 Spoon the tuna mayonnaise mixture into the tomato shells and garnish with sun-dried tomato strips and basil leaves. Return to the oven for a few minutes or serve chilled.

SERVES 4

4 plum tomatoes
2 tbsp sun-dried tomato paste
2 egg yolks
2 tsp lemon juice
finely grated rind of 1 lemon
4 tbsp olive oil
4 oz/115 g canned tuna, drained
2 tbsp capers, rinsed
salt and pepper

to garnish
2 sun-dried tomatoes, cut into strips
fresh basil leaves

NUTRITION
Calories *196*; Sugars *2 g*; Protein *9 g*;
Carbohydrate *2 g*; Fat *17 g*; Saturates *3 g*

⭐⭐ easy
🕐 5–10 mins
 25 mins

Fish *and* Seafood

Italians eat almost everything that comes out of the sea, from the tiny whitebait to the massive tuna fish. Fish markets in Italy are fascinating, with a huge variety of fish on display, but as most of the fish comes from the Mediterranean it is not always easy to find an equivalent elsewhere. However, fresh or frozen imported fish of all kinds is increasingly appearing in fish markets and supermarkets. After pasta, fish is probably the most important source of food in Italy, and in many recipes fish or seafood are served with one type of pasta or another— a winning combination!

Sea bass is a delicious white-fleshed fish. If cooking two small fish, they can be broiled; if cooking one large fish, bake it in the oven.

Baked Sea Bass

SERVES 4

3 lb/1.4 kg fresh sea bass or 2 sea bass about 1 lb 10 oz/750 g each, gutted
2–4 fresh rosemary sprigs
½ lemon, thinly sliced
2 tbsp olive oil
bay leaves and lemon wedges, to garnish

garlic sauce
2 tsp coarse sea salt
2 tsp capers
2 garlic cloves, crushed
4 tbsp water
2 fresh bay leaves
1 tsp lemon juice or wine vinegar
2 tbsp olive oil
pepper

NUTRITION
Calories *378*; Sugars *0 g*; Protein *62 g*;
Carbohydrate *0 g*; Fat *14 g*; Saturates *2 g*

challenging
15–20 mins
20–55 mins

1 Scrape off the scales from the fish and cut off the sharp fins. Make diagonal cuts along both sides. Wash and dry thoroughly. Place a rosemary sprig in the cavity of each of the smaller fish with half the lemon slices; or two sprigs and all the lemon in the large fish.

2 To broil: place in a foil-lined pan, brush with 1–2 tablespoons of oil and broil under a moderate heat for 5 minutes each side or until cooked through.

3 To bake: place the fish in a foil-lined dish or roasting pan brushed with oil, and brush the fish with the rest of the oil. Cook in a preheated oven, 375°F/190°C, for 30 minutes for the small fish or 45–50 minutes for the large fish, until the thickest part of the fish is opaque.

4 To make the sauce: crush the salt and capers with the garlic in a pestle and mortar and then work in the water. Or, work in a food processor or blender until smooth.

5 Bruise the bay leaves and remaining rosemary sprigs and put in a bowl. Add the garlic mixture, lemon juice and oil and pound together until the flavors are released. Season with pepper to taste.

6 Place the fish on a serving dish and, if liked, remove the skin. Spoon some of the sauce over the fish and serve the rest of the sauce separately. Garnish with fresh bay leaves and lemon wedges.

A rich wine and cream sauce makes this an excellent dinner party dish. You can make the bouillon the day before so it takes only minutes to cook and serve the fish.

Sole Fillets *in* Marsala *and* Cream

1 To make the bouillon, place the water, fish bones and skin, onion, carrot, and bay leaves in a pan and bring to a boil.

2 Reduce the heat and let the mixture simmer for 1 hour, or until the bouillon has reduced to about ⅔ cup. Drain the bouillon through a fine strainer, discarding the bones and vegetables, and set aside.

3 To make the sauce, heat the oil and butter in a skillet. Add the shallots and cook, stirring, for 2–3 minutes, or until just softened.

4 Add the mushrooms to the skillet and cook, stirring, for an additional 2–3 minutes, or until they are just beginning to brown.

5 Add the peppercorns and sole fillets to the skillet. Pan-fry the sole fillets for 3–4 minutes on each side, or until golden brown.

6 Pour the wine and bouillon over the fish and let simmer for 3 minutes. Remove the fish with a fish slice or a draining spoon, then set aside and keep warm.

7 Increase the heat and boil the mixture in the pan for about 5 minutes, or until the sauce has reduced and thickened.

8 Pour in the cream, then return the fish to the pan and heat through. Serve with cooked vegetables of your choice.

SERVES 4

bouillon
2½ cups water
bones and skin from the sole fillets
1 onion, halved
1 carrot, peeled and halved
3 fresh bay leaves

sauce
1 tbsp olive oil
1 tbsp butter
4 shallots, finely chopped
4 oz/100 g baby white mushrooms, wiped and halved
1 tbsp peppercorns, lightly crushed
8 sole fillets
⅓ cup Marsala wine
⅔ pint heavy cream
cooked vegetables, to serve

NUTRITION
Calories *474*; Sugars *3 g*; Protein *47 g*;
Carbohydrate *3 g*; Fat *28 g*; Saturates *14 g*

 challenging
15 mins
1 hr 30 mins

A delicious stuffing of sun-dried tomatoes and fresh lemon thyme are used to stuff whole sole.

Grilled Stuffed Sole

SERVES 4

1 tbsp olive oil
2 tbsp butter
1 small onion, chopped finely
1 garlic clove, chopped
3 sun-dried tomatoes, chopped
2 tbsp lemon thyme
1 cup bread crumbs
1 tbsp lemon juice
4 small whole sole, gutted and cleaned
salt and pepper
lemon wedges, to garnish
fresh salad greens, to serve

1 Heat the oil and butter in a skillet until it just begins to froth.

2 Add the onion and garlic to the skillet and cook, stirring, for 5 minutes, until just softened.

3 To make the stuffing, mix the tomatoes, thyme, bread crumbs, and lemon juice in a bowl, and season to taste.

4 Add the stuffing mixture to the pan, and stir to mix.

5 Using a sharp knife, pare the skin from the bone inside the gut hole of the fish to make a pocket. Spoon the tomato and herb stuffing into the pocket.

6 Cook the fish, under a preheated broiler, for 6 minutes on each side, or until golden brown.

7 Transfer the stuffed fish to serving plates and garnish with lemon wedges. Serve with fresh salad greens.

NUTRITION
Calories *207*; Sugars *0.2 g*; Protein *24 g*;
Carbohydrate *8 g*; Fat *10 g*; Saturates *4 g*

⭐⭐⭐ moderate
🕐 20 mins
🕐 15 mins

 COOK'S TIP

Lemon thyme (*Thymus* x *citriodorus*) has a delicate lemon scent and flavor. Ordinary thyme can be used instead, but mix it with 1 teaspoon of lemon peel to add extra flavor.

This delicate-tasting dish is surprisingly satisfying for even the largest appetites. Prepare the Italian Red Wine Sauce well in advance.

Lemon Sole *and* Haddock Ravioli

1 Flake the lemon sole and haddock fillets with a fork and transfer the flesh to a large mixing bowl.

2 Mix the eggs, cooked potato gnocchi, bread crumbs and cream in a bowl until thoroughly combined. Add the fish to the bowl containing the gnocchi and season the mixture with salt and pepper to taste.

3 Roll out the pasta dough on a lightly floured surface and cut out 3-inch/ 7.5-cm rounds using a plain cutter.

4 Place a spoonful of the fish stuffing on each round. Dampen the edges slightly and fold the pasta rounds over, pressing together to seal.

5 Bring a large pan of lightly salted water to the boil. Add the ravioli and cook for 15 minutes.

6 Drain the ravioli, using a draining spoon, and transfer to a large serving dish. Pour over the Italian Red Wine Sauce, sprinkle over the Parmesan cheese and serve immediately.

SERVES 4

1 lb/450 g lemon sole fillets, skinned
1 lb/450 g haddock fillets, skinned
3 eggs beaten
1 lb/450 g cooked potato gnocchi
3 cups fresh bread crumbs
¼ cup heavy cream
1 lb/450 g Basic Pasta Dough (see page 9)
1¼ cups Italian Red Wine Sauce (see page 15)
⅔ cup freshly grated Parmesan cheese
salt and pepper

NUTRITION
Calories *977*; Sugars *7 g*; Protein *67 g*;
Carbohydrate *93 g*; Fat *40 g*; Saturates *17 g*

 challenging

1 hr 40 mins

15 mins

This recipe from Trentino is best when the fish are freshly caught, but it is a good way to cook any trout, giving it an interesting flavor.

Trout *in* Red Wine

SERVES 4

4 fresh trout, about 10 oz/300 g each
1 cup red or white wine vinegar
1¼ cups red or dry white wine
⅔ cup water
1 carrot, sliced
2–4 bay leaves
thinly pared rind of 1 lemon
1 small onion, very thinly sliced
4 fresh parsley sprigs
4 fresh thyme sprigs
1 tsp black peppercorns
6–8 whole cloves
6 tbsp butter
1 tbsp chopped fresh mixed herbs
salt and pepper

to garnish
fresh parsley
lemon slices

NUTRITION
Calories *489*; Sugars *0.6 g*; Protein *48 g*;
Carbohydrate *0.6 g*; Fat *27 g*; Saturates *14 g*

challenging
30 mins
45 mins

1 Gut and clean the trout, but leave their heads on. Dry on paper towels and lay the fish head to tail in a shallow container or baking pan large enough to hold them.

2 Bring the wine vinegar to a boil and pour slowly all over the fish. Leave the fish to marinate in the refrigerator for about 20 minutes.

3 Meanwhile, put the wine, water, carrot, bay leaves, lemon rind, onion, herbs, peppercorns, and cloves into a pan with a good pinch of sea salt and heat through gently.

4 Drain the fish thoroughly, discarding the vinegar. Place the fish in a fish kettle or large skillet so they touch. When the wine mixture boils, strain gently over the fish so they are about half covered. Cover the pan and simmer very gently for 15 minutes.

5 Carefully remove the fish from the pan, draining off, but reserving, as much of the liquid as possible, and arrange the fish on a serving dish. Keep warm.

6 Boil the cooking liquid until reduced to about 4–6 tablespoons. Melt the butter in a pan and strain in the cooking liquor. Season and spoon the sauce over the fish. Garnish and serve.

Red mullet has a beautiful pink skin, which is enhanced in this dish by being cooked in red wine and orange juice.

Sardinian Red Mullet

1 Place the golden raisins in a bowl. Pour over the red wine and let soak for 10 minutes.

2 Heat the oil in a large skillet. Add the onions and sauté for 2 minutes.

3 Add the zucchini and cook for 3 minutes, or until tender.

4 Using a zester, pare long, thin strips from one of the oranges. Using a sharp knife, remove the peel from both of the oranges, then segment the oranges by slicing between the lines of pith.

5 Add the orange zest to the skillet. Add the red wine, golden raisins, red mullet, and anchovies to the pan and let simmer for 10–15 minutes, or until the fish is cooked through.

6 Stir in the oregano, then set aside and cool. Place the mixture in a large bowl and let chill, covered, in the refrigerator for at least 2 hours to let the flavors mingle. Transfer to serving plates and serve.

SERVES 4

½ cup golden raisins
⅔ cup red wine
2 tbsp olive oil
2 medium onions, sliced
1 zucchini cut into 2-inch/15-cm sticks
2 oranges
2 tsp coriander seeds, lightly ground
4 red mullet, boned and filleted
1¾ oz/50 g canned anchovy fillets, drained
2 tbsp chopped fresh oregano

NUTRITION

Calories *287*; Sugars *15 g*; Protein *31 g*;
Carbohydrate *15 g*; Fat *9 g*; Saturates *1 g*

⭐⭐⭐ moderate

🕐 2 hrs 30 mins

🕐 25 mins

 COOK'S TIP

Soaking the golden raisins in the red wine gives them an incredible flavor and succulence as they soak up all the wine.

Fresh salmon and pasta in a mouthwatering lemon and arugula sauce— a wonderful summer evening treat.

Salmon Steaks *with* Penne

SERVES 4

4 fresh salmon steaks
    about 10 oz/280 g each
4 tbsp butter
³/₄ cup dry white wine
sea salt
8 peppercorns
fresh dill sprig
fresh tarragon sprig
1 lemon, sliced
1 lb dried penne
2 tbsp olive oil

to garnish
lemon slices
arugula

lemon and arugula sauce
2 tbsp butter
¹/₄ cup all-purpose flour
⁵/₈ cup warm milk
juice and finely grated rind of 2 lemons
2 oz/55 g arugula, chopped
salt and pepper

NUTRITION
Calories *968*; Sugars *3 g*; Protein *59 g*;
Carbohydrate *49 g*; Fat *58 g*; Saturates *19 g*

        easy

        10 mins

        30 mins

1 Put the salmon in a large, non-slip pan. Add the butter, wine, a pinch of sea salt, the peppercorns, dill, tarragon, and lemon. Cover and bring to a boil, then simmer for 10 minutes.

2 Using a slice, carefully remove the salmon. Strain and reserve the cooking liquid. Remove and discard the salmon skin and center bones. Place on a warm dish, then cover and keep warm.

3 Meanwhile, bring a pan of salted water to a boil. Add the penne and 1 tablespoon of the oil and cook for 12 minutes, or until tender, but still firm to the bite. Drain and sprinkle over the remaining olive oil. Place on a warm serving dish and top with the salmon steaks, then keep warm.

4 To make the sauce, melt the butter and stir in the flour for 2 minutes. Stir in the milk and about 7 tablespoons of the reserved cooking liquid. Add the lemon juice and peel and cook, stirring, for an additional 10 minutes.

5 Add the arugula to the sauce and stir gently, then season to taste with salt and pepper.

6 Pour the sauce over the salmon and penne, then garnish with slices of lemon and arugula. Serve immediately.

Fresh tuna will be either a small bonito fish or steaks from a skipjack. The more delicately flavored fish have a paler flesh.

Tuna *with* Roast Bell Peppers

1 Put the tuna steaks into a large bowl with the lemon juice and water. Leave to marinate for 15 minutes.

2 Drain the tuna steaks and brush all over with olive oil and season well with salt and pepper.

3 Put the bell peppers over a hot barbecue or under a hot broiler and cook for 12 minutes until they are charred all over. Put them into a plastic bag and seal it.

4 Meanwhile, cook the tuna over a hot barbecue or broiler for 12–15 minutes, turning once.

5 When the bell peppers are cool enough to handle, peel them and cut each half into four strips. Toss them with the remaining olive oil, olives, and balsamic vinegar.

6 Serve the tuna steaks piping hot, with the roasted bell pepper salad.

SERVES 4

4 tuna steaks, about 9 oz/250 g each
3 tbsp lemon juice
4 cups water
6 tbsp olive oil
2 orange bell peppers, halved and seeded
2 red bell peppers, halved and seeded
12 black olives
1 tsp balsamic vinegar
salt and pepper

NUTRITION
Calories *428*; Sugars *5 g*; Protein *60 g*; Carbohydrate *5 g*; Fat *19 g*; Saturates *3 g*

  moderate

20 mins

30 mins

🍳 COOK'S TIP

Red, orange and yellow bell peppers can also be prepared by cooking them in a hot oven for 30 minutes, turning them frequently. Deseed the bell peppers after peeling.

You can substitute other whole fish for the snapper, such as cutlets of cod or halibut.

Baked Red Snapper

SERVES 4

juice of 2 limes, or 1 lemon
1 red snapper, about 2 lb 12 oz/1.25 kg, cleaned
4–5 fresh thyme or parsley sprigs
3 tbsp olive oil
1 large onion, chopped
2 garlic cloves, finely chopped
2 cups canned chopped tomatoes
2 tbsp tomato paste
2 tbsp red wine vinegar
5 tbsp unsweetened yogurt
2 tbsp chopped parsley
2 tsp dried oregano
6 tbsp dry bread crumbs
¼ cup low-fat yogurt cheese, crumbled
salt and pepper

to garnish
lime wedges
fresh dill sprigs

1 Sprinkle the lime or lemon juice inside and over the fish and season. Place the herbs inside the fish.

2 Heat the oil in a skillet and pan-fry the onion until translucent. Stir in the garlic and cook for 1 minute, then add the chopped tomatoes, tomato paste, and vinegar. Simmer, uncovered, for 5 minutes. Allow the sauce to cool, then stir in the yogurt, parsley, and oregano.

3 Pour half the sauce into an ovenproof dish just large enough for the fish. Add the fish then pour the remainder of the sauce over it, and sprinkle with bread crumbs. Bake uncovered for 30–35 minutes. Sprinkle the cheese over the fish and serve with lime wedges and dill sprigs.

NUTRITION
Calories *519*; Sugars *12 g*; Protein *61 g*; Fat *23 g*; Carbohydrate *18 g*; Saturates *3 g*

moderate

20 mins

50 mins

Marinating fish, for even a short period, adds a subtle flavor to the flesh and makes even simply broiled or pan-fried fish a delicious dish.

Marinated Fish

1 Using a sharp knife, cut 4–5 diagonal slashes on each side of the fish. Place the fish in a shallow, nonmetallic dish.

2 To make the marinade, mix together the marjoram, olive oil, lime peel and juice, garlic, and salt and pepper in a bowl.

3 Pour the marinade mixture over the fish. Leave to marinate in the refrigerator for 30 minutes.

4 Cook the mackerel, under a preheated broiler, for 5–6 minutes on each side, brushing occasionally with the reserved marinade, until golden.

5 Transfer the fish to serving plates. Pour over any remaining marinade before serving, garnished with lime wedges and with salad leaves.

SERVES 4

4 whole mackerel, cleaned and gutted
4 tbsp chopped fresh marjoram
2 tbsp extra-virgin olive oil
finely grated peel and juice of 1 lime
2 garlic cloves, finely chopped
salt and pepper
lime wedges, to garnish
green salad leaves, to serve

NUTRITION
Calories 361; Sugars 0 g; Protein 26 g; Carbohydrate 0 g; Fat 29 g; Saturates 5 g

   moderate
🕐   45 mins
🕐   15 mins

COOK'S TIP

If the lime is too hard to squeeze, microwave on high power for 30 seconds to release the juice. This dish is also excellent cooked on the barbecue.

This adaptation of an eighteenth-century Italian dish is baked until it is golden brown and sizzling, then cut into wedges like a cake.

Macaroni *and* Prawn Bake

SERVES 4

3 cups dried short-cut macaroni
1 tbsp olive oil, plus extra for brushing
6 tbsp butter, plus extra for greasing
2 small fennel bulbs, thinly sliced and fronds reserved
3 cups mushrooms, thinly sliced
6 oz/175 g peeled, cooked shrimp
pinch of cayenne pepper
1¼ cups Béchamel Sauce (see page 14)
⅔ cup freshly grated Parmesan cheese
2 large tomatoes, sliced
1 tsp dried oregano
salt and pepper

1 Bring a pan of salted water to a boil. Add the pasta and oil and cook until tender, but still firm to the bite. Drain and return to the pan. Add 2 tablespoons of butter, then cover and shake the pan. Keep warm.

2 Melt the remaining butter in a skillet. Pan-fry the fennel for 3–4 minutes. Stir in the mushrooms and cook for an additional 2 minutes. Stir in the shrimp, then remove the skillet from the heat.

3 Stir the cayenne pepper and shrimp mixture into the Béchamel sauce. Pour into a greased ovenproof dish and spread out evenly. Sprinkle over the Parmesan cheese and arrange the tomato slices in a ring around the edge. Brush the tomatoes with olive oil and sprinkle over the oregano.

4 Bake in a preheated oven at 350°F/180°C, for 25 minutes, until golden brown. Serve immediately.

NUTRITION
Calories *478*; Sugars *6 g*; Protein *27 g*; Carbohydrate *57 g*; Fat *17 g*; Saturates *7 g*

 moderate

20 mins

45 mins

🍴 COOK'S TIP
This dish can be made in advance, then kept in the refrigerator or it may be frozen without the tomatoes, and cooked when required.

Popular in fishing ports around Europe, gentle stewing is an excellent way to maintain the flavor and succulent texture of fish and shellfish.

Mediterranean Fish Stew

1 Heat the oil in a large non-stick saucepan and cook the onions and garlic gently for 3 minutes.

2 Stir in the vinegar and sugar and cook for a further 2 minutes.

3 Stir in the bouillon, wine, tomatoes, eggplant, zucchini, bell pepper, and rosemary. Bring to a boil and simmer, uncovered, for 10 minutes.

4 Slice the squid into rings, add the halibut, mussels and squid. Mix well and simmer, covered, for 5 minutes until the fish is opaque.

5 Stir in the shrimp and continue to simmer, covered, for a further 2–3 minutes until the shrimp are pink and cooked through.

6 Discard any mussels which haven't opened and season to taste.

7 To serve, put a slice of the prepared garlic bread in the base of each warmed serving bowl and ladle the stew over the top. Serve with lemon wedges.

SERVES 4

2 tbsp olive oil
2 red onions, sliced
2 garlic cloves, crushed
2 tbsp red wine vinegar
2 tsp superfine sugar
1¼ cups Fresh Fish Bouillon (see page 16)
1¼ cups dry red wine
4 cups canned chopped tomatoes
8 oz/225 g baby eggplant, quartered
8 oz/225 g yellow zucchini, sliced
1 green bell pepper, sliced
1 tbsp chopped fresh rosemary
1 lb 2 oz/500 g halibut fillet, skinned and cut into 1-inch/2.5-cm cubes
1 lb 10 oz/750 g fresh mussels, prepared
8 oz/225 g baby squid, cleaned,trimmed
8 oz/225 g fresh tiger shrimp, prepared
salt and pepper
4 slices toasted French bread rubbed with a cut garlic clove
lemon wedges, to serve

NUTRITION

Calories 533; Sugars 11 g; Protein 71 g; Carbohydrate 30 g; Fat 10 g; Saturates 2 g

✪✪✪✪ challenging

🕐 1 hr

🕐 25 mins

This flavorsome, colorful fish pie is perfect for a light supper. The addition of smoked salmon gives it a touch of luxury.

Smoky Fish Pie

SERVES 4

2 lb/900 g smoked haddock or cod fillets
2½ cups skim milk
2 bay leaves
4 oz/115 g white mushrooms, quartered
1 cup frozen peas
⅔ cup frozen corn kernels
4 cups diced potatoes
5 tbsp unsweetened plain yogurt
4 tbsp chopped fresh parsley
2 oz/55 g smoked salmon, sliced
   into thin strips
3 tbsp cornstarch
¼ cup grated smoked cheese
salt and pepper

NUTRITION
Calories 523; Sugars 15 g; Protein 58 g;
Carbohydrate 63 g; Fat 6 g; Saturates 2 g

 challenging

🕐 15 mins

🕐 1 hr

1 Place the fish in a large pan and add the milk and bay leaves. Bring to a boil, cover, and then simmer gently for 5 minutes.

2 Add the mushrooms, peas, and corn, bring back to a simmer, cover, and cook for 5–7 minutes. Let cool.

3 Place the potatoes in a pan, cover with water, bring to a boil, and cook for 8 minutes. Drain well and mash with a fork or a potato masher. Stir in the yogurt and parsley and season to taste with salt and pepper. Set aside.

4 Using a draining spoon, remove the fish from the pan. Flake the cooked fish away from the skin and place the fish in an ovenproof gratin dish. Reserve the cooking liquid.

5 Drain the vegetables, reserving the cooking liquid, and gently stir into the fish with the salmon strips.

6 Blend a little cooking liquid into the cornstarch to make a paste. Transfer the rest of the liquid to a pan and add the paste. Heat through, stirring, until thickened. Discard the bay leaves and season to taste. Pour the sauce over the fish and vegetables and mix. Spoon over the mashed potato so that the fish is covered, sprinkle with cheese, and bake in a preheated oven, 400°F/200°C, for 25–30 minutes.

Use smoked cod or haddock in this delicious lasagna. It's a great way to make a little go a long way.

Smoked Fish Lasagna

1 Heat the oil in a pan and cook the garlic and onion for about 5 minutes. Add the mushrooms and cook for 3 minutes, stirring.

2 Add the tomatoes, zucchini, and bouillon or water and simmer, uncovered, for 15–20 minutes until the vegetables are soft. Season.

3 Put the butter or margarine, milk, and flour into a small saucepan and heat, whisking constantly, until the sauce boils and thickens. Remove from the heat and add half of the cheese and all of the parsley. Stir gently to melt the cheese and season to taste.

4 Spoon the tomato sauce mixture into a large, shallow ovenproof dish and top with half of the lasagne sheets. Scatter the chunks of fish evenly over the top, then pour over half of the cheese sauce. Top with the remaining lasagna sheets and then spread the rest of the cheese sauce on top. Sprinkle with the remaining cheese.

5 Bake in a preheated oven, at 375°F/190°C, for 40 minutes, until the top is golden brown and bubbling. Garnish with parsley sprigs and serve hot.

S E R V E S 4

2 tsp olive or vegetable oil
1 garlic clove, crushed
1 small onion, finely chopped
2 cups mushrooms, sliced
2 cups canned chopped tomatoes
1 small zucchini, sliced
²⁄₃ cup vegetable bouillon or water
2 tbsp butter or margarine
1¼ cups skim milk
¼ cup all-purpose flour
1 cup grated sharp colby cheese
1 tbsp chopped fresh parsley
6 sheets precooked lasagna
12 oz/350 g skinned and boned smoked cod or haddock, cut into chunks
salt and pepper
fresh parsley sprigs, to garnish

N U T R I T I O N
Calories *483*; Sugars *8 g*; Protein *36 g*;
Carbohydrate *32 g*; Fat *24 g*; Saturates *12 g*

✪✪✪   moderate
◔   20 mins
🕐   1 hr 15 mins

 C O O K ' S   T I P

You can use almost any variety of fish in this recipe but smoked fish adds a very special flavor.

This is the ideal dish when you have unexpected guests because the parcels can be prepared in advance, then put in the oven when you are ready to eat.

Pasta *and* Shrimp Parcels

SERVES 4

1 lb/450 g dried fettuccine
⅝ cup Pesto Sauce (see page 133)
4 tsp extra-virgin olive oil
1 lb 10 oz/750 g large raw shrimp, peeled and deveined
2 garlic cloves, crushed
½ cup dry white wine
salt and pepper

1 Cut out 4 x 12-inch/30-cm squares of greaseproof paper.

2 Bring a large pan of lightly salted water to a boil. Add the fettuccine and cook for 2–3 minutes, until just softened. Drain and set aside.

3 Mix together the fettuccine and half of the Pesto Sauce. Spread out the paper squares and put 1 teaspoon of olive oil in the middle of each. Divide the fettuccine between the squares, then divide the shrimp and place on top of the fettuccine.

4 Mix together the remaining Pesto Sauce and the garlic and spoon it over the shrimp. Season each parcel with salt and pepper and sprinkle with the white wine.

5 Dampen the edges of the greaseproof paper and wrap the parcels loosely, twisting the edges to seal.

6 Place the parcels on a cookie sheet and bake in a preheated oven, at 400°F/200°C, for 10–15 minutes. Transfer the parcels to individual serving plates and serve.

NUTRITION

Calories *640*; Sugars *1 g*; Protein *50 g*;
Carbohydrate *42 g*; Fat *29 g*; Saturates *4 g*

 moderate

 20 mins

20 mins

🍲 **COOK'S TIP**

Traditionally, these parcels are designed to look like money bags. The resemblance is more effective with greaseproof paper than with foil.

A luxurious dish which makes an impressive appetizer or light meal, shrimp and garlic are a winning combination.

Pan-Fried Shrimp

1 Wash the shrimp and pat dry using paper towels.

2 Melt the butter with the oil in a large skillet, add the garlic and shrimp, and cook over a high heat, stirring, for 3–4 minutes until the shrimp are pink.

3 Sprinkle with brandy and season with salt and pepper to taste. Sprinkle with parsley and serve immediately with lemon wedges and ciabatta bread.

SERVES 4

4 garlic cloves, peeled and sliced
20–24 unshelled large raw shrimp
½ cup butter
4 tbsp olive oil
6 tbsp brandy
salt and pepper
2 tbsp chopped fresh parsley

to serve
lemon wedges
ciabatta bread

NUTRITION
Calories *455*; Sugars *0 g*; Protein *6 g*;
Carbohydrate *0 g*; Fat *37 g*; Saturates *18 g*

 very easy

10 mins

5 mins

Whole squid are stuffed with a mixture of fresh herbs and sun-dried tomatoes and then cooked in a wine sauce.

Squid *with* Wine *and* Rosemary

SERVES 4

8 squid, cleaned and gutted, but left whole
6 canned anchovies, chopped
2 garlic cloves, chopped
2 tbsp chopped rosemary leaves
2 sun-dried tomatoes, chopped
5½/150 g bread crumbs
1 tbsp olive oil
1 onion, finely chopped
¾ cup white wine
¾ cup Fish Bouillon (see page 16)
cooked rice, to serve

1 Remove the tentacles from the body of the squid and chop the flesh finely.

2 Grind the anchovies, garlic, rosemary and tomatoes to a paste in a mortar and pestle.

3 Add the bread crumbs and the chopped squid tentacles and mix. If the mixture is too dry to form a thick paste at this point, add about 1 teaspoon of water.

4 Spoon the paste into the body sacs of the squid, then tie a length of cotton around the end of each sac to fasten. Do not overfill the sacs, because the filling will expand during cooking.

5 Heat the oil in a skillet. Add the onion and cook, stirring, for 3–4 minutes, or until golden.

6 Add the stuffed squid to the pan and cook for 3–4 minutes, or until they are brown all over.

7 Add the wine and Fish Bouillon and bring to the boil. Reduce the heat, cover, and then leave to simmer for 15 minutes.

8 Remove the lid and cook for a further 5 minutes, or until the squid is tender and the juices reduced. Serve with cooked rice.

NUTRITION

Calories 276; Sugars 1 g; Protein 23 g; Carbohydrate 20 g; Fat 8 g; Saturates 1 g

✪✪✪   moderate

🕐   25 mins

🕐   35 mins

This is one of those dishes that looks almost too lovely to eat—but you must!

Farfallini Buttered Lobster

1 Carefully discard the stomach sac, vein, and gills from each lobster. Remove all the meat from the tail and chop. Crack the claws and legs, then remove the meat and chop. Transfer the meat to a bowl and add the lemon juice and grated lemon peel.

2 Clean the shells thoroughly and place in a warm oven, at 325°F/160°C, to dry out.

3 Melt 2 tablespoons of the butter in a skillet. Add the bread crumbs and cook for about 3 minutes, or until crisp and golden brown.

4 Melt the remaining butter in a pan. Add the lobster meat and heat through gently. Add the brandy and cook for an additional 3 minutes, add the cream, and season to taste with salt and pepper.

5 Meanwhile, bring a large pan of lightly salted water to a boil. Add the farfallini and olive oil and cook for about 12 minutes, or until tender, but still firm to the bite. Drain and spoon the pasta into the clean lobster shells. Top with the buttered lobster and sprinkle with a little grated Parmesan cheese and the bread crumbs. Broil for 2–3 minutes, or until golden brown.

6 Transfer the lobster shells to a warm serving dish. Garnish with the lemon slices, kiwi fruit, jumbo shrimp, and dill sprigs and serve immediately.

SERVES 4

1½ lb/700 g lobsters, split into halves
juice and grated peel of 1 lemon
½ cup butter
4 tbsp fresh white bread crumbs
2 tbsp brandy
5 tbsp heavy cream
1 lb/450 g dried farfallini
1 tbsp olive oil
⅔ cup freshly grated Parmesan cheese
salt and pepper

to garnish
1 kiwi fruit, sliced
4 unshelled cooked jumbo shrimp
fresh dill sprigs

NUTRITION
Calories *686*; Sugars *1 g*; Protein *45 g*;
Carbohydrate *44 g*; Fat *36 g*; Saturates *19 g*

✪✪✪   moderate

        30 mins

        25 mins

A quickly cooked recipe that transforms pantry ingredients into a dish with style.

Vermicelli *with* Clams

SERVES 4

14 oz/400 g dried vermicelli, spaghetti or other long pasta
2 tbsp olive oil
2 tbsp butter
2 onions, chopped
2 garlic cloves, chopped
2 x 7 oz jars clams in brine
½ cup white wine
4 tbsp chopped fresh parsley
½ tsp dried oregano
pinch of freshly grated nutmeg
salt and pepper

to garnish
2 tbsp Parmesan cheese shavings
fresh basil sprigs

1 Bring a large pan of lightly salted water to a boil. Add the pasta and half the olive oil and cook until tender, but still firm to the bite. Drain, then return to the pan and add the butter. Cover the pan and shake well. Keep warm.

2 Heat the remaining oil in a pan over a medium heat. Add the onions and cook until they are translucent. Stir in the garlic and cook for 1 minute.

3 Strain the liquid from 1 jar of clams and add the liquid to the pan, with the wine. Stir, then bring to simmering point and simmer for 3 minutes. Drain the second jar of clams and discard the liquid.

4 Add the clams, parsley, and oregano to the pan and season with pepper and nutmeg. Lower the heat and cook until the sauce is heated through.

5 Transfer the pasta to a warm serving dish and pour over the sauce. Sprinkle with the Parmesan cheese and garnish with the basil. Serve at once.

NUTRITION
Calories *520*; Sugars *2 g*; Protein *26 g*;
Carbohydrate *71 g*; Fat *13 g*; Saturates *4 g*

 easy
10 mins
25 mins

 COOK'S TIP

There are many different types of clams found along almost every coast in the world. Those traditionally used in this dish are the tiny ones— only 1–2 in/ 2.5–5 cm across—known in Italy as *vongole*.

This is another tempting seafood dish where the eye is delighted as much as the taste buds.

Baked Scallops *with* Pasta in Shells

1 Remove the scallops from their shells. Scrape off the skirt and the black intestinal thread. Reserve the white part (the flesh) and the orange part (the coral or roe). Very carefully ease the flesh and coral from the shell with a short, but very strong knife.

2 Wash the shells thoroughly and dry them well. Put the shells on a cookie sheet. Sprinkle lightly with about two-thirds of the olive oil and set aside.

3 Meanwhile, bring a large pan of lightly salted water to a boil. Add the pasta shells and remaining olive oil and cook for about 12 minutes, or until tender, but still firm to the bite. Drain and spoon about 1 oz/25 g of pasta into each scallop shell.

4 Put the scallops, fish bouillon and onion in an ovenproof dish and season to taste with pepper. Cover with foil and bake in a preheated oven at 350°F/180°C, for 8 minutes.

5 Remove the dish from the oven. Remove the foil and, using a draining spoon, transfer the scallops to the shells. Add 1 tablespoon of the cooking liquid to each shell, together with a drizzle of lemon juice, a little lemon peel, and a little cream, then top with the grated cheese.

6 Increase the oven temperature to 450°F/230°C and return the scallops to the oven for an additional 4 minutes.

7 Serve the scallops in their shells with crusty brown bread and butter.

SERVES 4

12 scallops
3 tbsp olive oil
3 cups small, dried whole-wheat pasta shells
5/8 cup Fish Bouillon (see page 16)
1 onion, chopped
juice and finely grated peel of 2 lemons
5/8 cup heavy cream
2 cups grated hard cheese
salt and pepper
crusty brown bread, to serve

NUTRITION
Calories *725*; Sugars *2 g*; Protein *38 g*; Carbohydrate *38 g*; Fat *48 g*; Saturates *25 g*

　moderate

　20 mins

　30 mins

Meat

Italians have their very own special way of butchering meat, producing very different cuts. Most meat is sold ready-boned and often cut straight across the grain. Veal is a great favorite and widely available. Pork is also popular, with roast pig being the traditional dish of Umbria. Suckling pig is roasted with lots of fresh herbs, especially rosemary, until the skin is crisp and brown. Lamb is often served for special occasions, cooked on a spit or roasted in the oven with wine, garlic, and herbs; and the very small cutlets from young lambs feature widely, especially in Rome. Variety meats play an important role, too, with liver, brains, sweetbreads, tongue, heart, tripe, and kidneys always available. Whatever your favorite Italian meat dish is, it's sure to be included in this chapter.

Barolo is a famous wine from the Piedmont area of Italy. Its mellow flavor is the key to this dish, so don't stint on the quality of the wine.

Beef *in* Barolo

SERVES 4

4 tbsp oil

2 lb 4 oz/1 kg piece boned rolled rib of beef, or piece of silverside

2 garlic cloves, crushed

4 shallots, sliced

1 tsp chopped fresh rosemary

1 tsp chopped fresh oregano

2 celery stalks, sliced

1 large carrot, diced

2 whole cloves

1 bottle Barolo wine

freshly grated nutmeg

salt and pepper

cooked vegetables, such as broccoli, carrots, and new potatoes, to serve

1 Heat the oil in a flameproof casserole and brown the meat all over. Remove the meat from the casserole.

2 Add the garlic, shallots, herbs, celery, carrot, and cloves and pan-fry for 5 minutes.

3 Replace the meat on top of the vegetables. Pour in the wine. Cover the casserole and simmer gently for about 2 hours until tender. Remove the meat from the casserole, slice and keep warm.

4 Rub the contents of the pan through a strainer or purée in a blender, adding a little hot beef stock if necessary. Season with nutmeg, salt and pepper.

5 Serve the meat with the sauce and accompanied by cooked vegetables, such as broccoli, carrots, and new potatoes, if wished.

NUTRITION

Calories 744; Sugars 1 g; Protein 66 g; Carbohydrate 1 g; Fat 43 g; Saturates 16 g

moderate

15 mins

2 hrs 15 mins

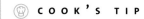 **COOK'S TIP**

If Barolo is unavailable choose another full-bodied red wine instead.

Wafer-thin slices of tender beef with a rich garlic and bacon stuffing, flavored with the tang of orange.

Beef Olives *in* Rich Gravy

1 Unroll the beef olives and flatten out as thinly as possible using a meat tenderizer or mallet. Trim the edges to neaten them.

2 Mix together the parsley, garlic, bacon, orange rind, and salt and pepper. Spread this mixture evenly over each beef olive.

3 Roll up each beef olive tightly, then secure with a toothpick. Heat the oil in a skillet and pan-fry the beef on all sides for 10 minutes.

4 Drain the beef olives, reserving the pan juices, and keep warm. Pour the wine into the juices, add the bay leaf, sugar, and seasoning. Bring to a boil and boil rapidly for 5 minutes to reduce slightly, stirring.

5 Return the cooked beef to the pan along with the black olives and heat through for a further 2 minutes. Discard the bay leaf and toothpicks.

6 Transfer the beef olives and gravy to a serving dish, and serve garnished with orange slices and parsley.

SERVES 4

8 ready-prepared beef olives
4 tbsp chopped fresh parsley
4 garlic cloves, finely chopped
8–10 strips smoked streaky bacon, rinded and finely chopped
grated rind of ½ small orange
2 tbsp olive oil
1¼ cups dry red wine
1 bay leaf
1 tsp sugar
16–18 pitted black olives, drained
salt and pepper

to garnish
orange slices
chopped fresh parsley

NUTRITION
Calories *379*; Sugars *4 g*; Protein *26 g*;
Carbohydrate *4 g*; Fat *24 g*; Saturates *8 g*

⭐⭐⭐   moderate
🕐   20 mins
🕐   20 mins

In this recipe the "pasta" dough is made with potatoes instead of the traditional flour. The ravioli are filled with a rich bolognese sauce.

Beef *and* Potato Ravioli

SERVES 4

filling
1 tbsp vegetable oil
½ cup ground beef
1 shallot, diced
1 garlic clove, crushed
1 tbsp all-purpose flour
1 tbsp tomato paste
⅔ cup beef bouillon
1 celery stalk, chopped
2 tomatoes, peeled and diced
2 tsp chopped fresh basil
salt and pepper

ravioli
2⅔ cups diced mealy potatoes
3 small egg yolks
3 tbsp olive oil
1½ cups all-purpose flour
5 tbsp butter, for frying
shredded fresh basil leaves, to garnish

NUTRITION
Calories *618*; Sugars *4 g*; Protein *16 g*;
Carbohydrate *74 g*; Fat *31 g*; Saturates *12 g*

challenging
30 mins
50 mins

1 To make the filling, heat the oil in a pan and cook the beef for 3–4 minutes, breaking it up with a spoon. Add the shallot and garlic and cook for 2–3 minutes until the shallot has softened.

2 Stir in the flour and tomato paste and cook for 1 minute. Stir in the beef bouillon, celery, tomatoes, and the chopped fresh basil. Season to taste with salt and pepper.

3 Cook the mixture over a low heat for 20 minutes. Remove from the heat and let cool.

4 To make the ravioli, cook the potatoes in a pan of boiling water for 10 minutes until cooked.

5 Mash the potatoes in a mixing bowl. Add the egg yolks and oil. Season, then stir in the flour and mix to form a dough.

6 On a lightly floured surface, divide the dough into 24 pieces and shape into flat rounds. Spoon the filling on to one half of each round and fold the dough over to encase the filling, pressing down to seal the edges.

7 Melt the butter in a skillet and cook the ravioli for 6–8 minutes, turning once, until golden. Serve hot, garnished with shredded basil leaves.

A different twist is given to this traditional pasta dish with a rich, but subtle sauce.

Meatballs *in* Red Wine Sauce

1 Pour the milk into a bowl and soak the bread crumbs in the milk for 30 minutes.

2 Heat half of the butter and 4 tablespoons of the oil in a pan. Pan-fry the mushrooms for 4 minutes, then stir in the flour and cook for 2 minutes. Add the bouillon and wine and simmer for 15 minutes. Add the tomatoes, tomato paste, sugar, and basil. Season and simmer for 30 minutes.

3 Mix the shallots, steak, and paprika with the breadcrumbs and season to taste. Shape the mixture into 14 meatballs.

4 Heat 4 tablespoons of the remaining oil and the remaining butter in a large skillet. Pan-fry the meatballs, turning frequently, until brown all over. Transfer to a deep casserole, pour over the red wine and the mushroom sauce, cover and bake in a preheated oven, at 350°F/180°C, for 30 minutes.

5 Bring a pan of salted water to a boil. Add the pasta and the remaining oil and cook for 8–10 minutes or until tender. Drain and transfer to a serving dish. Remove the casserole from the oven and cool for 3 minutes. Pour the meatballs and sauce onto the pasta, garnish with basil sprigs and serve.

SERVES 4

⅔ cup milk
2 cups white bread crumbs
2 tbsp butter
4 fl oz/135 ml olive oil
3 cups sliced oyster mushrooms
¼ cup whole-wheat flour
⅞ cup beef bouillon
⅔ cup red wine
4 tomatoes, peeled and chopped
1 tbsp tomato paste
1 tsp brown sugar
1 tbsp finely chopped fresh basil
12 shallots, chopped
4 cups ground steak
1 tsp paprika
1 lb/450 g dried egg tagliarini
salt and pepper
fresh basil sprigs, to garnish

COOK'S TIP

Choose a good quality, full-bodied red wine for this recipe, for extra flavor.

NUTRITION
Calories *811*; Sugars *7 g*; Protein *30 g*;
Carbohydrate *76 g*; Fat *43 g*; Saturates *12 g*

⭐⭐⭐   moderate
             45 mins
             1 hr 40 mins

The fresh taste of sage is the perfect ingredient to counteract the richness of pork in this quick and simple dish.

Pork Chops *with* Sage

SERVES 4

2 tbsp flour
1 tbsp chopped fresh sage or 1 tsp dried
4 lean boneless pork chops, trimmed of excess fat
2 tbsp olive oil
1 tbsp butter
2 red onions, sliced into rings
1 tbsp lemon juice
2 tsp superfine sugar
4 plum tomatoes, quartered
salt and pepper
salad leaves, to serve

1 Mix the flour, sage, and salt and pepper on a plate. Lightly dust the pork chops on both sides with the seasoned flour.

2 Heat the oil and butter in a frying pan, then add the chops and cook them for 6–7 minutes on each side, or until cooked through. Drain the chops, reserving the pan juices, and keep warm.

3 Toss the onion in the lemon juice and fry along with the sugar and tomatoes for 5 minutes, or until tender.

4 Serve the pork with the tomato and onion mixture and a green salad.

NUTRITION
Calories *364*; Sugars *5 g*; Protein *34 g*;
Carbohydrate *14 g*; Fat *19 g*; Saturates *7 g*

  easy

10 mins

15 mins

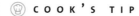 **COOK'S TIP**

If plum tomatoes are unavailable choose ripe, but firm large tomatoes instead.

This traditional dish of boned pork cooked with garlic and milk can be served hot or cold.

Pork Cooked *in* Milk

1 Using a sharp knife, remove the fat from the pork. Shape the meat into a neat form, tying it in place with a length of string.

2 Heat the oil and butter in a large pan. Add the onion, garlic, and pancetta to the pan and cook for 2–3 minutes.

3 Add the pork to the pan and cook, turning occasionally, until it is browned.

4 Pour over the milk, add the peppercorns, bay leaves, marjoram, and thyme and cook over a low heat for 1¼–1½ hours or until tender. Watch the liquid carefully for the last 15 minutes of cooking time because it tends to reduce very quickly and will then burn. If the liquid reduces and the pork is still not tender, add another 5–7 tablespoons milk and continue cooking. Reserve the cooking liquid (as the milk reduces naturally in this dish, it forms a thick and creamy sauce, which curdles slightly, but tastes very delicious).

5 Remove the pork from the pan. Using a sharp knife, cut the meat into slices. Transfer the pork slices to serving plates and serve immediately with the reserved cooking liquid.

SERVES 4

1¾ lb/800 g leg of pork, boned
1 tbsp oil
2 tbsp butter
1 onion, chopped
2 garlic cloves, chopped
¾ cup diced pancetta
5 cups milk
1 tbsp green peppercorns, crushed
2 fresh bay leaves
2 tbsp fresh marjoram
2 tbsp fresh thyme

NUTRITION
Calories *498*; Sugars *15 g*; Protein *50 g*;
Carbohydrate *15 g*; Fat *27 g*; Saturates *9 g*

 moderate

 20 mins

 1 hr 45 mins

This is a simplified version of a traditional dish from the Marche region, on the east coast of Italy. Pork fillet pockets are stuffed with prosciutto and herbs.

Pork *with* Lemon *and* Garlic

SERVES 4

1 lb/450 g pork fillet
2/3 cup chopped almonds
2 tbsp olive oil
4 oz Parma ham, finely chopped
2 garlic cloves, chopped
1 tbsp fresh oregano, chopped
finely grated rind of 2 lemons
4 shallots, finely chopped
3/4 cup ham or chicken bouillon
1 tsp sugar

1 Using a sharp knife, cut the pork fillet into 4 equal pieces. Place the pork between sheets of oiled paper and pound each piece with a meat mallet or the end of a rolling pin to flatten it.

2 Cut a horizontal slit in each piece of pork to make a pocket.

3 Place the almonds on a baking sheet. Lightly toast the almonds under a medium–hot broiler for 2–3 minutes, or until golden.

4 Mix the almonds with 1 tablespoon of the olive oil, chopped Parma ham, garlic, oregano, and the finely grated rind from 1 lemon. Spoon the mixture into the pockets of the pork.

5 Heat the remaining olive oil in a large skillet. Add the shallots and cook for 2 minutes.

6 Add the pork to the skillet and cook for 2 minutes on each side, or until browned all over.

7 Add the bouillon to the pan and bring to a boil. Cover and let simmer for 45 minutes, or until the pork is tender. Remove the meat from the pan, then set aside and keep warm.

8 Using a zester, pare the remaining lemon. Add the peel and sugar to the pan, then boil for 3–4 minutes, or until reduced and syrupy. Pour over the pork fillets and serve immediately.

NUTRITION
Calories *428*; Sugars *2 g*; Protein *31 g*; Carbohydrate *4 g*; Fat *32 g*; Saturates *4 g*

★★★ moderate

🕐 25 mins

🕐 1 hr

This sophisticated roast with Mediterranean flavors is ideal served with a pungent olive paste and a salad.

Pork Stuffed *with* Prosciutto

1 Trim away the excess fat and membrane from the pork fillet. Slice the pork lengthwise down the middle, taking care not to cut all the way through.

2 Open out the pork and season the inside. Lay the basil leaves down the center of the pork. Mix the cheese and sun-dried tomato paste and spread over the basil.

3 Press the pork fillet back together. Wrap the Parma ham around the stuffed pork, overlapping it, to cover. Place it on a rack in a roasting pan, seamside down, and brush with oil. Bake in a preheated oven, 375°F/190°C, for 30–40 minutes depending on thickness, until cooked through. Allow the pork to stand for 10 minutes before serving.

4 To make the olive paste, place all the ingredients in a blender or a food processor and blend until smooth. For a coarser paste, finely chop the olives and garlic and mix with the oil.

5 Drain the cooked stuffed pork and slice it thinly. Serve it with the olive paste and an attractive salad.

SERVES 4

1 lb 2 oz/450 g piece of lean pork fillet
small bunch fresh basil leaves, washed
2 tbsp freshly grated Parmesan cheese
2 tbsp sun-dried tomato paste
6 thin slices Parma ham (prosciutto)
1 tbsp olive oil
salt and pepper
salad leaves, to serve

olive paste
1 cup pitted black olives
4 tbsp olive oil
2 garlic cloves, peeled

COOK'S TIP

Choose a good lean piece of pork fillet for the best results.

NUTRITION
Calories *427*; Sugars *0 g*; Protein *31 g*;
Carbohydrate *0.2 g*; Fat *34 g*; Saturates *7 g*

 moderate

25 mins

55 mins

Cannelloni, the thick, round pasta tubes, make perfect containers for close-textured sauces of all kinds.

Spinach, Cheese *and* Ham Cannelloni

SERVES 4

8 dried cannelloni tubes
1 tbsp olive oil
⅓ cup freshly grated Parmesan cheese
fresh herb sprigs, to garnish

filling

2 tbsp butter
10½ oz/300 g frozen spinach, thawed
    and chopped
½ cup ricotta cheese
⅓ cup freshly grated Parmesan cheese
¼ cup chopped ham
pinch of freshly grated nutmeg
2 tbsp heavy cream
2 eggs, lightly beaten
salt and pepper

sauce

2 tbsp butter
scant ¼ cup all-purpose flour
1¼ cups milk
2 bay leaves
pinch of freshly grated nutmeg

NUTRITION

Calories 520; Sugars 5 g; Protein 21 g;
Carbohydrate 23 g; Fat 39 g; Saturates 18 g

  moderate

🕐 30 mins

🕐 1 hr 15 mins

1 To make the filling, melt the butter in a pan over low heat and cook the spinach for 2–3 minutes. Remove from the heat and stir in the ricotta, Parmesan cheese, and the ham. Season to taste with nutmeg and salt and pepper. Beat in the cream and eggs to make a thick paste.

2 Bring a pan of lightly salted water to a boil. Add the pasta and the oil, return to a boil, and cook for 10–12 minutes or until tender, but still firm to the bite. Drain and let cool.

3 To make the sauce, melt the butter in a pan. Stir in the flour and cook, stirring, for 1 minute. Gradually stir in the milk. Add the bay leaves and simmer, stirring, for 5 minutes. Add the nutmeg and salt and pepper to taste. Remove from the heat and discard the bay leaves.

4 Spoon the filling into a pastry bag and use to fill the cannelloni.

5 Spoon a little sauce into the base of an ovenproof dish. Arrange the cannelloni in the dish in a single layer and pour over the remaining sauce. Sprinkle over the Parmesan cheese and bake in a preheated oven, 375°F/190°C, for 40–45 minutes. Garnish and serve.

An Italian version of broiled pork steaks, this dish is easy to make and delicious to eat.

Neapolitan Pork Steaks

1 Heat the oil in a large skillet. Add the onion and garlic and cook, stirring, for 3–4 minutes, or until they are just beginning to soften.

2 Add the tomatoes and yeast extract to the skillet and let simmer for about 5 minutes, or until the sauce starts to thicken.

3 Cook the pork steaks, under a preheated broiler, for 5 minutes on both sides, or until the the meat is golden and cooked through. Set the pork steaks aside and keep warm.

4 Add the olives and fresh shredded basil to the sauce in the skillet and stir quickly to combine.

5 Transfer the steaks to warm serving plates. Top the steaks with the sauce and sprinkle with freshly grated Parmesan cheese, and serve at once with vegetables of your choice.

SERVES 4

2 tbsp olive oil
1 large onion, sliced
1 garlic clove, chopped
2 cups canned tomatoes
2 tsp yeast extract
4 pork loin steaks, about 4½ oz/125 g each
¾ cup black olives, pitted
2 tbsp fresh basil, shredded

to serve
freshly grated Parmesan cheese
fresh vegetables

NUTRITION
Calories 353; Sugars 3 g; Protein 39 g;
Carbohydrate 4 g; Fat 20 g; Saturates 5 g

⭐⭐ easy
🕐 10 mins
🕐 25 mins

 COOK'S TIP

Parmesan cheese is a mature and exceptionally hard cheese produced in Italy. You only need to add a little as it has a very strong flavor.

Chunks of tender lamb, pan-fried with garlic and stewed in red wine, are a traditional Roman dish.

Lamb *and* Anchovies *with* Thyme

SERVES 4

1 tbsp oil
1 tbsp butter
1 ½ lb/700 g lamb (shoulder or leg), cut into 1-inch/2.5-cm chunks
4 garlic cloves, peeled
3 fresh thyme sprigs, stalks removed
6 canned anchovy fillets
⅔ cup red wine
⅔ cup lamb or vegetable bouillon
1 tsp sugar
16 black olives, pitted and halved
2 tbsp chopped fresh parsley, to garnish

1 Heat the oil and butter in a large skillet. Add the lamb and cook for 4–5 minutes, stirring, until the meat is browned all over.

2 Using a pestle and mortar, grind together the garlic, thyme, and anchovies to make a smooth paste.

3 Add the wine and bouillon to the skillet. Stir in the garlic and anchovy paste together with the sugar.

4 Bring the mixture to a boil, reduce the heat, cover, and leave to simmer for 30–40 minutes or until the lamb is tender. For the last 10 minutes of the cooking time, remove the lid in order to let the sauce reduce slightly.

5 Stir the olives into the sauce and mix to combine.

6 Transfer the lamb and the sauce to a serving bowl and garnish with chopped fresh parsley.

NUTRITION

Calories *299*; Sugars *1 g*; Protein *31 g*;
Carbohydrate *1 g*; Fat *16 g*; Saturates *7 g*

★★★   moderate
🕐   15 mins
🕐   50 mins

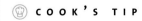 COOK'S TIP

This dish is excellent served with mashed or lightly sautéed potatoes.

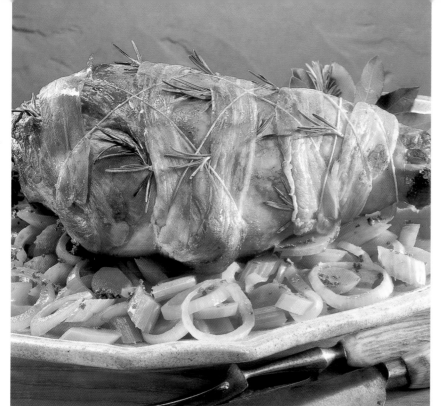

This dish from the Abruzzi region of Italy uses a slow cooking method. The meat absorbs the flavorings and becomes very tender.

Pot Roasted Leg *of* Lamb

1 Wipe the joint of lamb all over, trimming off any excess fat, then season with salt and pepper, rubbing well in. Lay the sprigs of rosemary over the lamb, cover evenly with the bacon strips, and tie in place with string.

2 Heat the oil in a skillet and pan-fry the lamb for about 10 minutes, turning several times. Remove from the skillet.

3 Transfer the oil from the skillet to a large flameproof casserole and cook the garlic and onion for 3–4 minutes until beginning to soften. Add the carrots and celery and cook for a few minutes longer.

4 Lay the lamb on top of the vegetables and press down to partly submerge. Pour the wine over the lamb, add the tomato paste, and simmer for about 3–4 minutes. Add the bouillon, tomatoes, and herbs and season to taste with salt and pepper. Bring back to a boil for a further 3–4 minutes.

5 Cover the casserole tightly and cook in a moderate oven, 350°F/180°C, for 2–2½ hours until very tender.

6 Remove the lamb from the casserole and if preferred, take off the bacon and herbs along with the string. Keep warm. Strain the juices, skimming off any excess fat, and serve in a pitcher. The vegetables may be arranged around the pot roast or in a serving dish. Garnish with fresh rosemary sprigs.

SERVES 4

3 ½ lb/1.6 kg leg of lamb
3–4 fresh rosemary sprigs
8–10 bacon strips
4 tbsp olive oil
2–3 garlic cloves, crushed
2 onions, sliced
2 carrots, sliced
2 celery stalks, sliced
1¼ cups dry white wine
1 tbsp tomato paste
1¼ cups vegetable bouillon
4 tomatoes, peeled, cut into fourths, and seeded
1 tbsp chopped fresh parsley
1 tbsp chopped fresh oregano or marjoram
salt and pepper
fresh rosemary sprigs, to garnish

NUTRITION
Calories 734; Sugars 6 g; Protein 71 g;
Carbohydrate 7 g; Fat 42 g; Saturates 15 g

 challenging

35 mins

3 hrs

A classic combination of flavors, this dish would make a perfect Sunday lunch. Serve with tomato and onion salad and jacket potatoes.

Lamb Cutlets *with* Rosemary

SERVES 4

8 lamb cutlets
5 tbsp olive oil
2 tbsp lemon juice
1 garlic clove, finely chopped
½ tsp lemon pepper
salt
8 fresh rosemary sprigs
jacket potatoes, to serve

salad

4 tomatoes, sliced
4 scallions, sliced diagonally

dressing

2 tbsp olive oil
1 tbsp lemon juice
1 garlic clove, chopped
¼ tsp finely chopped fresh rosemary

1 Trim the lamb chops by cutting away the flesh with a sharp knife to expose the tips of the bones.

2 Place the oil, lemon juice, garlic, lemon pepper, and salt in a shallow, non-metallic dish and whisk with a fork to combine.

3 Lay the sprigs of rosemary in the dish and place the lamb on top. Leave to marinate for at least 1 hour, turning the lamb cutlets once.

4 Remove the chops from the marinade and wrap a little kitchen foil around the tips of the bones to stop them from burning.

5 Place the sprigs of rosemary on the rack and place the lamb on top. Broil for 10–15 minutes, turning once.

6 Meanwhile, make the salad and dressing. Arrange the tomatoes on a serving dish and scatter the scallions on top. Place all the ingredients for the dressing in a screw-top jar, shake well and pour over the salad. Serve with the broiled lamb cutlets and jacket potatoes.

NUTRITION

Calories *560*; Sugars *1 g*; Protein *48 g*; Carbohydrate *1 g*; Fat *40 g*; Saturates *1 g*

⭐⭐⭐ moderate
🕐 1 hr 15 mins
🕐 15 mins

 **COOK'S TIP**

Choose medium to small baking potatoes if you want to cook jacket potatoes on the grill. Scrub them well, prick with a fork and wrap in buttered kitchen foil. Bury them in the hot coals and chargrill for 50–60 minutes.

These lamb chops
become more elegant
when the bone is removed
to make noisettes.

Lamb *with* Bay *and* Lemon

1 Using a sharp knife, carefully remove the bone from each lamb chop, keeping the meat intact. Alternatively, ask the butcher to prepare the lamb noisettes for you.

2 Shape the meat into rounds and secure with a length of string.

3 In a large skillet, heat together the oil and butter until it starts to froth.

4 Add the lamb noisettes to the skillet and cook for 2–3 minutes on each side or until browned all over.

5 Remove the skillet fom the heat, remove the lamb, drain off all of the excess fat, and discard. Return the meat to the skillet.

6 Return the skillet to the heat. Add the wine, bouillon, bay leaves and lemon rind to the skillet and cook for 20–25 minutes or until the lamb is tender. Season the lamb noisettes and sauce to taste with a little salt and pepper.

7 Transfer to serving plates. Remove the string from each noisette and serve with the sauce.

SERVES 4

4 lamb chops
1 tbsp oil
1 tbsp butter
⅔ cup white wine
⅔ cup lamb or vegetable bouillon
2 bay leaves
pared rind of 1 lemon
salt and pepper

NUTRITION
Calories *268*; Sugars *0.2 g*; Protein *24 g*;
Carbohydrate *0.2 g*; Fat *16 g*; Saturates *7 g*

✪✪✪   moderate

🕐   10 mins

🕐   35 mins

The Italian name for this dish literally means "jump into the mouth" because it is so delicious. The stuffed rolls are quick and easy to make.

Saltimbocca

SERVES 4

4 turkey fillets or 4 veal escalopes, about 1 lb/450 g in total
4 oz/115 g prosciutto
8 fresh sage leaves
1 tbsp olive oil
1 onion, chopped finely
3/4 cup white wine
3/4 cup chicken bouillon

1 Place the turkey or veal between sheets of waxed paper. Pound the meat with a meat mallet or the end of a rolling pin to flatten it slightly. Cut each escalope in half.

2 Trim the prosciutto to fit each piece of turkey or veal and place over the meat. Lay a sage leaf on top. Roll up the escalopes and secure with a wooden toothpick.

3 Heat the oil in a skillet and cook the onion for 3–4 minutes. Add the turkey or veal rolls to the pan and cook for 5 minutes, or until brown all over.

4 Pour the wine and bouillon into the pan and let simmer for 15 minutes if using turkey, and 20 minutes for veal, or until tender. Serve immediately.

NUTRITION
Calories *303*; Sugars *0.3 g*; Protein *29 g*; Carbohydrate *1 g*; Fat *17 g*; Saturates *1 g*

  moderate

15 mins

25–30 mins

COOK'S TIP

If using turkey rather than veal, watch it carefully as turkey tends to turn dry very quickly if overcooked.

The delicious combination of apple, onion, and mushroom perfectly complements the delicate flavor of veal.

Neapolitan Veal Cutlets *and* Mascarpone

1 Melt 4 tablespoons of the butter in a skillet. Cook the veal over a low heat for 5 minutes on each side. Transfer to a dish and keep warm.

2 Cook the onion and apples in the skillet, until lightly browned. Transfer to a dish, then place the veal on top and keep warm.

3 Melt the remaining butter in the skillet. Gently cook the mushrooms, tarragon, and peppercorns over a low heat for 3 minutes. Sprinkle over the sesame seeds.

4 Bring a pan of salted water to a boil. Add the pasta and 1 tablespoon of the oil. Cook until tender, but still firm to the bite. Drain, transfer to a serving plate, and keep warm.

5 Top the pasta with the mascarpone and sprinkle over the remaining olive oil. Place the onions, apples, and veal cutlets on top of the pasta. Spoon the mushrooms and peppercorns on to the cutlets, then place the tomatoes and basil leaves around the edge. Place in a preheated oven, at 300°F/150°C, for 5 minutes.

6 Season to taste with salt and pepper, then garnish with fresh basil leaves, and serve immediately.

SERVES 4

⅞ cup butter
4 trimmed veal cutlets,
    each about 9 oz/250 g
1 large onion, sliced
2 apples, peeled, cored, and sliced
6 oz/175 g white mushrooms
1 tbsp chopped fresh tarragon
8 black peppercorns
1 tbsp sesame seeds
14 oz/400 g dried marille pasta
scant ½ cup extra-virgin olive oil
¾ cup mascarpone cheese
salt and pepper
2 large beefsteak tomatoes, halved
1 sprig of fresh basil leaves, plus extra
    to garnish

NUTRITION
Calories *1071*; Sugars *13 g*; Protein *74 g*;
Carbohydrate *66 g*; Fat *59 g*; Saturates *16 g*

✪✪✪   moderate

      20 mins

       30 mins

This dish is delicious if made with tender veal. However, if veal is unavailable, use pork or turkey escalopes instead.

Veal Italienne

SERVES 4

5 tbsp butter
1 tbsp olive oil
1 lb 8 oz/675 g potatoes, cubed
4 veal escalopes, about 6 oz/175 g each
1 onion, cut into 8 wedges
2 garlic cloves, crushed
2 tbsp all-purpose flour
2 tbsp tomato paste
²/₃ cup red wine
1¼ cups chicken bouillon
8 ripe tomatoes, peeled, seeded, and diced
8–9 pitted black olives, halved
2 tbsp chopped fresh basil
salt and pepper
fresh basil leaves, to garnish

1 Heat the butter and oil in a large skillet. Add the potato cubes and cook for 5–7 minutes, stirring frequently, until they begin to brown.

2 Remove the potatoes from the skillet with a slotted spoon and set aside.

3 Place the veal in the skillet and cook for 2–3 minutes on each side until sealed. Remove from the pan and then set aside.

4 Stir the onion and garlic into the skillet and cook for 2–3 minutes.

5 Add the flour and tomato paste and cook for 1 minute, stirring. Gradually blend in the red wine and chicken bouillon, stirring to make a smooth sauce.

6 Return the potatoes and veal to the skillet. Stir in the tomatoes, olives, and chopped basil and season with salt and pepper.

7 Transfer to a casserole dish and cook in a preheated oven, 350°F/180°C, for 1 hour or until the potatoes and veal are cooked through. Garnish with fresh basil leaves and serve.

NUTRITION
Calories 592; Sugars 5 g; Protein 44 g;
Carbohydrate 48 g; Fat 23 g; Saturates 9 g

⭐⭐⭐   moderate
🕐   25 mins
🕐   1 hr 20 mins

 COOK'S TIP

For a quicker cooking time and really tender meat, pound the meat with a meat mallet or the end of a rolling pin to flatten it slightly before cooking.

Anchovies are often used to enhance flavor, particularly in meat dishes.

Escalopes *and* Italian Sausage

1 Heat the oil in a large skillet. Add the anchovies, capers, fresh rosemary, grated orange rind and juice, Italian sausage, and tomatoes to the pan and cook for 5–6 minutes, stirring occasionally.

2 Meanwhile, place the turkey or veal escalopes between sheets of greaseproof paper. Pound the meat with a meat mallet or the end of a rolling pin in order to flatten it.

3 Add the escalopes to the mixture in the skillet. Season to taste with salt and pepper, cover and cook for 3–5 minutes on each side, slightly longer if the meat is thicker.

4 Transfer to serving plates and serve with fresh crusty bread.

SERVES 4

1 tbsp olive oil
6 canned anchovy fillets, drained
1 tbsp capers, drained
1 tbsp fresh rosemary leaves
finely grated rind and juice of 1 orange
3 oz/75 g Italian sausage, diced
3 tomatoes, peeled and chopped
4 turkey or veal escalopes, about
    4 oz/100 g each
salt and pepper
crusty bread or cooked polenta, to serve

NUTRITION
Calories *233*; Sugars *1 g*; Protein *28 g*;
Carbohydrate *1 g*; Fat *13 g*; Saturates *1 g*

 COOK'S TIP

Try using 4-minute steaks, slightly flattened, instead of the turkey or veal. Cook them for 4–5 minutes on top of the sauce in the pan.

⭐⭐   easy
🕐   10 mins
🕐   20 mins

In this traditional Tuscan dish, Italian sausages are cooked with cannellini beans and tomatoes.

Sausage *and* Bean Casserole

SERVES 4

8 Italian sausages
1 tbsp olive oil
1 large onion, chopped
2 garlic cloves, chopped
1 green bell pepper, halved, seeded, and cut into strips
8 oz fresh tomatoes, peeled and chopped or 2 cups chopped canned tomatoes
2 tbsp sun-dried tomato paste
1 ½ cups cannellini beans
mashed potato or rice, to serve

1 Prick the Italian sausages all over with a fork. Cook them, under a preheated broiler, for 10–12 minutes, turning occasionally, until brown all over. Set aside and keep warm.

2 Heat the oil in a large skillet. Add the onion, garlic, and bell pepper to the skillet and cook for 5 minutes, stirring occasionally, or until softened.

3 Add the tomatoes to the skillet and let the mixture simmer for about 5 minutes, stirring occasionally, or until slightly reduced and thickened.

4 Stir the sun-dried tomato paste, cannellini beans, and Italian sausages into the mixture in the skillet. Cook for 4–5 minutes, or until the mixture is piping hot. Add 4–5 tablespoons of water, if the mixture becomes too dry during cooking.

5 Transfer the Italian sausage and bean casserole to serving plates and serve with mashed potato or rice.

NUTRITION
Calories *600*; Sugars *7 g*; Protein *27 g*; Carbohydrate *20 g*; Fat *47 g*; Saturates *16 g*

easy
15 mins
35 mins

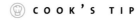 **COOK'S TIP**

Italian sausages are coarse in texture and have a strong flavor. They can be found in specialist sausage stores, Italian delicatessens, and some larger supermarkets. They are replaceable in this recipe only by game sausages.

Liver is popular in Italy and is served in many ways. Tender calf's liver is the best type to use for this recipe, but you could use lamb's liver.

Liver *with* Wine Sauce

1 Wipe the liver with paper towels, season with salt and pepper to taste and then coat lightly in flour, shaking off any excess.

2 Heat the oil and butter in a skillet and pan-fry the liver until well sealed on both sides and just cooked through—take care not to overcook. Remove the liver from the skillet, cover and keep warm, but do not allow to dry out.

3 Add the bacon to the fat left in the skillet, with the garlic, onion, and celery. Cook gently until soft.

4 Add the red wine, beef bouillon, allspice, Worcestershire sauce, sage, and salt and pepper to taste. Bring to the boil and simmer for 3–4 minutes.

5 Cut each tomato segment in half. Add to the sauce and continue to cook for 2–3 minutes.

6 Serve the liver on a little of the sauce, with the remainder spooned over. Garnish with fresh sage leaves and serve with new or sauté potatoes.

SERVES **4**

4 slices calf's liver or 8 slices lamb's liver, about 1 lb/450 g
flour, for coating
1 tbsp olive oil
2 tbsp butter
8–10 strips lean back bacon, de-rinded, and cut into narrow slivers
1 garlic clove, crushed
1 onion, chopped
1 celery stalk, thinly sliced
⅔ cup red wine
⅔ cup beef bouillon
good pinch of ground allspice
1 tsp Worcestershire sauce
1 tsp chopped fresh sage or ½ tsp dried sage
3–4 tomatoes, peeled, cut into fourths and seeded
salt and pepper
fresh sage leaves, to garnish
new potatoes or sauté potatoes, to serve

NUTRITION
Calories *435*; Sugars *2 g*; Protein *30 g*; Carbohydrate *4 g*; Fat *31 g*; Saturates *12 g*

⭐⭐⭐   moderate

🕐   25 mins

🕐   20 mins

Chicken *and* Poultry

Poultry dishes provide some of Italy's finest food. Every part of the chicken is used, including the feet and innards for making soup. Spit-roasted chicken, strongly flavored with aromatic rosemary, has become almost a national dish. Turkey, capon, duck, goose, and guinea fowl are also popular, as is game. Wild rabbit, hare, wild boar and deer are available, especially in Sardinia. This chapter contains a superb collection of mouthwatering recipes. You will be astonished at how quickly and easily you can prepare some of these gourmet dishes.

A roast that is full of Mediterranean flavor. A mixture of feta cheese, rosemary, and sun-dried tomatoes is stuffed under the chicken skin, then roasted with garlic, new potatoes, and vegetables.

Mediterranean-Style Chicken

SERVES 4

5 lb 8 oz/2.5 kg whole chicken
fresh rosemary sprigs
¾ cup feta cheese, coarsely grated
2 tbsp sun-dried tomato paste
4 tbsp butter, softened
pepper
1 garlic bulb
2 lb 4 oz/1 kg new potatoes, halved if large
1 each red, green, and yellow bell pepper, halved, seeded, and cut into chunks
3 zucchini, thinly sliced
2 tbsp olive oil
2 tbsp all-purpose flour
2½ cups chicken bouillon

NUTRITION

Calories *488*; Sugars *6 g*; Protein *37 g*; Carbohydrate *34 g*; Fat *23 g*; Saturates *11 g*

moderate

35 mins

1 hr 30 mins

1 Rinse the chicken inside and out with cold water and drain well. Carefully cut between the skin and the top of the breast meat using a small pointed knife. Slide a finger into the slit and carefully enlarge it to form a pocket. Continue until the skin is completely lifted away from both breasts and the top of the legs.

2 Chop the leaves from 3 rosemary sprigs. Mix with the feta, sun-dried tomato paste, butter, and pepper then spoon under the skin. Put the chicken in a large roasting pan, cover with foil, and cook in a preheated oven, 375°F/190°C, for 20 minutes per 1 lb/450 g, plus 20 minutes.

3 Break the garlic bulb into cloves, but do not peel. Add the vegetables to the chicken in the pan after 40 minutes.

4 Drizzle with oil, tuck in a few rosemary sprigs, and season well. Cook for the remaining time, removing the foil for the last 40 minutes of cooking to brown the chicken.

5 Transfer the chicken to a serving platter. Place some of the vegetables around the chicken and transfer the remainder to a warmed serving dish. Pour the fat out of the roasting pan and stir the flour into the remaining pan juices. Cook for 2 minutes then gradually stir in the bouillon. Bring to a boil, stirring until thickened. Strain into a sauce boat and serve with the chicken and vegetables.

There is a delicious surprise of creamy garlic and herb cheese inside these chicken breast packets!

Garlic *and* Herb Chicken

1 Using a sharp knife, make a horizontal slit along the length of each chicken breast to form a pocket.

2 Beat the cheese with a wooden spoon to soften it. Spoon the cheese into the pocket of the chicken breasts.

3 Wrap 2 slices of Parma ham around each chicken breast and secure in place with string.

4 Pour the wine and chicken bouillon into a large skillet and bring to a boil. When the mixture is just starting to boil, add the sugar and stir to dissolve.

5 Add the chicken breasts to the mixture in the skillet. Let simmer for 12–15 minutes, or until the chicken is tender and the juices run clear when a skewer is inserted into the thickest part of the meat.

6 Remove the chicken from the skillet, then set aside and keep warm.

7 Reheat the sauce and boil until reduced and thickened. Remove the string from the chicken and cut into slices. Pour the sauce over the chicken and serve with salad.

SERVES 4

4 chicken breasts, skin removed
3½ oz/90 g full-fat soft cheese, flavored with herbs and garlic
8 slices Parma ham
⅔ cup red wine
⅔ cup chicken bouillon
1 tbsp brown sugar
salad leaves, to serve

NUTRITION
Calories 272; Sugars 4 g; Protein 29 g; Carbohydrate 4 g; Fat 13 g; Saturates 6 g

moderate

20 mins

25 mins

COOK'S TIP

Try adding 2 finely chopped sun-dried tomatoes to the soft cheese in step 2, if you prefer.

This dish combines succulent chicken with tasty vegetables, flavored with wine and olives.

Chicken *with* Vegetables

SERVES 4

4 chicken breasts, part boned
2 tbsp butter
2 tbsp olive oil
1 large onion, finely chopped
2 garlic cloves, crushed
2 bell peppers, red, yellow or green, halved, seeded and cut into large pieces
8 oz/225 g large closed cup mushrooms, sliced or quartered
2–3 tomatoes, peeled and halved
2/3 cup dry white wine
1–1 1/2 cups green olives, pitted
4–6 tbsp heavy cream
salt and pepper
pasta, to serve
chopped fresh flatleaf parsley, to garnish

1 Season the chicken with salt and pepper to taste. Heat the oil and butter in a skillet, add the chicken and fry until browned all over. Remove the chicken from the skillet.

2 Add the onion and garlic to the skillet and cook gently until just beginning to soften. Add the bell peppers to the skillet with the mushrooms and continue to cook for a few minutes longer, stirring occasionally.

3 Add the tomatoes and plenty of seasoning to the skillet and then transfer the vegetable mixture to an ovenproof casserole. Place the chicken on the bed of vegetables.

4 Add the wine to the skillet and bring to a boil. Pour the wine over the chicken and cover the casserole tightly. Cook in a preheated oven, 350°F/180°C, for 50 minutes.

5 Add the olives to the chicken, mix lightly then pour on the cream. Re-cover the casserole and return to the oven for 10–20 minutes or until the chicken is very tender.

6 Adjust the seasoning and serve the pieces of chicken, surrounded by the vegetables and sauce, with pasta or tiny new potatoes. Sprinkle with chopped parsley to garnish.

NUTRITION

Calories *470*; Sugars *7 g*; Protein *29 g*; Carbohydrate *7 g*; Fat *34 g*; Saturates *16 g*

moderate

20 mins

1 hr 30 mins

This casserole is packed with the sunshine flavors of Italy. Sun-dried tomatoes add a wonderful richness to the dish.

Rich Chicken Casserole

1 In a large, heavy skillet, cook the chicken without fat over a fairly high heat, turning occasionally until golden brown. Using a drainage spoon, drain off any excess fat from the chicken and transfer to a flameproof casserole.

2 Add the olive oil to the pan and cook the onion, garlic, and bell pepper over a moderate heat for 3–4 minutes. Transfer to the casserole.

3 Add the orange rind and juice, chicken bouillon, chopped tomatoes, and sun-dried tomatoes to the casserole and stir to combine.

4 Bring to a boil, then cover the casserole with a lid and simmer very gently over a low heat for about 1 hour, stirring occasionally. Add the chopped fresh thyme and pitted black olives, then adjust the seasoning with salt and pepper to taste.

5 Scatter orange rind and thyme over the casserole to garnish, and serve with crusty bread.

SERVES 4

8 chicken thighs
2 tbsp olive oil
1 medium red onion, sliced
2 garlic cloves, crushed
1 large red bell pepper, thickly sliced
thinly pared rind and juice of 1 small orange
½ cup chicken bouillon
2 cups canned chopped tomatoes
½ cup sun-dried tomatoes, sliced thinly
1 tbsp chopped fresh thyme
16–18 pitted black olives
salt and pepper

to garnish
orange rind
thyme sprigs

to serve
crusty fresh bread

NUTRITION
Calories *320*; Sugars *8 g*; Protein *34 g*;
Carbohydrate *8 g*; Fat *17 g*; Saturates *4 g*

✪✪✪ moderate
 15 mins
🕐 1 hr 15 mins

👨‍🍳 COOK'S TIP

Sun-dried tomatoes have a dense texture and concentrated taste, and add intense flavor to slow-cooking casseroles.

Strips of cooked chicken are tossed with colored pasta, grapes, and carrot sticks in a delicious pesto-flavored dressing.

Pasta *and* Chicken Medley

S E R V E S   4

generous 1–1⅓ cups dried pasta shapes, such as twists or bows
1 tbsp olive oil
2 tbsp mayonnaise
2 tsp bottled pesto sauce
1 tbsp sour cream
6 oz/175 g cooked skinless, boneless chicken meat, cut into strips
1–2 celery stalks, cut diagonally into slices
16–18 black grapes (preferably seedless), halved, reserving a few whole, to garnish
1 large carrot, cut into julienne strips
salt and pepper
celery leaves, to garnish

dressing
1 tsp white wine vinegar
1 tbsp extra-virgin olive oil
salt and pepper

1 To make the dressing, whisk all the ingredients together until smooth.

2 Bring a large pan of lightly salted water to a boil. Add the pasta, and oil, bring back to a boil, and cook for 8–10 minutes until tender, but still firm to the bite. Drain thoroughly, rinse, and drain again. Transfer to a bowl and mix in the dressing while still hot, then set aside until cold.

3 Combine the mayonnaise, pesto sauce, and sour cream in a bowl and season to taste with salt and pepper.

4 Add the chicken, celery, grapes, carrot, and mayonnaise mixture to the pasta and toss thoroughly. Taste and adjust the seasoning, adding more salt and pepper if necessary.

5 Arrange the pasta mixture on 2 plates and garnish with the reserved whole black grapes and celery leaves.

N U T R I T I O N
Calories *609*; Sugars *11 g*; Protein *26 g*; Carbohydrate *45 g*; Fat *38 g*; Saturates *6 g*

    moderate

30 mins

10 mins

This method of cooking makes the chicken aromatic and succulent. It also reduces the amount of oil needed since the chicken and vegetables cook in their own juices.

Italian Chicken Parcels

1 Cut 6 pieces of foil to about 10 inches/25 cm square. Brush the foil squares lightly with oil and set aside until required.

2 With a sharp knife, make slashes at intervals across each chicken breast, then slice the mozzarella cheese and place between the cuts in the chicken.

3 Divide the zucchini and tomatoes between the pieces of foil and sprinkle with pepper. Tear or roughly chop the basil and scatter over the vegetables in each packet.

4 Place the chicken on top of each pile of vegetables then wrap in the foil to enclose the chicken and vegetables, tucking in the ends.

5 Place on a cookie sheet and bake in a preheated oven, 400°F/200°C, for about 30 minutes.

6 To serve, unwrap each foil parcel and serve with pasta or rice.

SERVES 4

1 tbsp olive oil
6 skinless chicken breast fillets
2 cups mozzarella cheese
3½ cups sliced zucchini
6 large tomatoes, sliced
pepper
1 small bunch fresh basil or oregano
pasta or rice, to serve

NUTRITION
Calories 234; Sugars 5 g; Protein 28 g;
Carbohydrate 5 g; Fat 12 g; Saturates 5 g

⊛⊛   easy
🕐   25 mins
🕐   30 mins

 COOK'S TIP

Place the vegetables and chicken on the shiny side of the foil so, once the packet is wrapped up, the dull surface faces outward. This ensures that the heat is absorbed into the packet and not reflected away from it.

This classic Roman dish makes an ideal light meal. It is equally good cold and could be taken on a picnic – serve with bread to mop up the juices.

Roman Chicken

SERVES 4

4 tbsp olive oil

6 chicken pieces

2 garlic cloves, crushed with 1 tsp salt

1 large red onion, sliced

4 large mixed red, green and yellow bell
    peppers, seeded and cut into strips

1 cup pitted green olives

½ quantity Basic Tomato Sauce (see page 14)

1¼ cups hot chicken bouillon

2 fresh marjoram sprigs

salt and pepper

crusty bread, to serve

1 Heat half of the oil in a flameproof casserole and brown the chicken pieces on all sides. Remove the chicken and set aside.

2 Add the remaining oil to the casserole and pan-fry the garlic and onion until softened. Stir in the bell peppers, olives, and Basic Tomato Sauce.

3 Return the chicken to the casserole with the bouillon and marjoram. Cover the casserole and simmer for about 45 minutes, or until the chicken is tender. Season with salt and pepper to taste and serve with crusty bread.

NUTRITION

Calories *317*; Sugars *8 g*; Protein *22 g*;
Carbohydrate *9 g*; Fat *22 g*; Saturates *4 g*

moderate

35 mins

1 hr

All the sunshine colors and flavors of the Mediterranean are combined in this easy dish.

Chicken Pepperonata

1 Remove the skin from the chicken thighs and toss in the flour.

2 Heat the oil in a wide skillet and pan-fry the chicken quickly until sealed and lightly browned, then remove from the pan. Add the onion to the pan and gently pan-fry until soft. Add the garlic, bell peppers, tomatoes, and oregano, then bring to a boil, stirring.

3 Arrange the chicken over the vegetables, then season well with salt and pepper. Cover the skillet tightly and simmer for 20–25 minutes, or until the chicken is completely cooked and tender.

4 Adjust the seasoning, if necessary, garnish with oregano and serve with crusty whole-wheat bread.

SERVES 4

8 skinless chicken thighs
2 tbsp whole-wheat flour
2 tbsp olive oil
1 small onion, sliced thinly
1 garlic clove, minced
1 each large red, yellow, and green bell
    peppers, sliced thinly
2 cups canned chopped tomatoes
1 tbsp chopped fresh oregano
salt and pepper
fresh oregano, to garnish
crusty whole-wheat bread, to serve

NUTRITION
Calories 328; Sugars 7 g; Protein 35 g;
Carbohydrate 13 g; Fat 15 g; Saturates 4 g

easy

15 mins

40 mins

🍲 **COOK'S TIP**

For extra flavor, halve the peppers and broil under a preheated broiler until the skins are charred. Let cool, then remove the peel and seeds. Thinly slice the bell peppers and use in the recipe.

The refreshing combination of chicken and orange sauce makes this a perfect dish for a warm summer evening.

Chicken *with* Orange Sauce

SERVES 4

2 tbsp canola oil
2 tbsp olive oil
4 chicken breasts, about 8 oz/225 g each, boned and skinned
2/3 cup orange brandy
2 tbsp all-purpose flour
2/3 cup freshly squeezed orange juice
1/4 cup zucchini, cut into thin batons
1 quarter red bell pepper, cut into thin batons
6 tbsp finely shredded leek
14 oz/400 g dried whole-wheat spaghetti
3 large oranges, peeled and cut into segments
rind of 1 orange, cut into very fine strips
2 tbsp chopped fresh tarragon
2/3 cup ricotta cheese
salt and pepper
fresh tarragon leaves, to garnish

1 Heat the canola oil and 1 tablespoon of the olive oil in a skillet. Add the chicken and cook over fairly high heat until golden brown. Add the orange brandy and cook for 3 minutes. Sprinkle in the flour and cook, stirring constantly, for 2 minutes.

2 Lower the heat and add the orange juice, zucchini, red bell pepper, and leek and season to taste. Simmer for 5 minutes until the sauce has thickened.

3 Meanwhile, bring a pan of lightly salted water to a boil. Add the spaghetti, bring back to a boil, and cook for 10 minutes until tender, but still firm to the bite. Drain the spaghetti, transfer to a warmed serving dish, and drizzle over the remaining oil.

4 Add half of the orange segments, half of the orange rind, the tarragon, and ricotta cheese to the sauce in the pan and cook for 3 minutes.

5 Place the chicken on top of the pasta, pour over a little sauce, garnish with orange segments, rind, and tarragon. Serve immediately with extra sauce.

NUTRITION
Calories 797; Sugars 28 g; Protein 59 g; Carbohydrate 77 g; Fat 25 g; Saturates 6 g

 moderate
 15 mins
15 mins
25 mins

🍳 **COOK'S TIP**

You could use cointreau or brandy in place of the orange brandy if it is unavailable.

Stuffed with creamy ricotta, nutmeg, and spinach, the chicken is then wrapped with wafer-thin slices of prosciutto and gently cooked in wine.

Cheese-stuffed Chicken *in* Wine

1 Put the spinach into a strainer and press out the water with a spoon. Mix with the ricotta and nutmeg and season with salt and pepper to taste.

2 Using a sharp knife, slit each chicken breast through the side and enlarge each cut to form a pocket. Fill with the spinach mixture, then reshape the chicken breasts. Wrap each breast tightly in a slice of Parma ham and secure with toothpicks. Cover and chill in the refrigerator.

3 Heat the butter and oil in a skillet and brown the chicken breasts for 2 minutes on each side. Transfer the chicken to a large, shallow ovenproof dish and keep warm until required.

4 Cook the onions and mushrooms for 2–3 minutes, until lightly browned. Stir in the all-purpose flour, then gradually add the wine and bouillon. Bring to a boil, stirring constantly. Season and spoon the mixture around the chicken.

5 Cook the chicken uncovered in a preheated oven, 400°F/200°C, for 20 minutes. Turn the breasts over and cook for an additional 10 minutes. Remove the toothpick and serve with the sauce, together with carrot purée and green beans, if wished.

SERVES 4

½ cup frozen spinach, thawed
½ cup ricotta cheese
pinch grated nutmeg
4 skinless, boneless chicken breasts, about 6 oz/175 g each
4 Parma ham slices
2 tbsp butter
1 tbsp olive oil
12 small onions or shallots
1½ cups white mushrooms, sliced
1 tbsp all-purpose flour
⅔ cup dry white or red wine
1¼ cups chicken bouillon
salt and pepper

to serve
carrot purée
fine beans

NUTRITION
Calories *426*; Sugars *4 g*; Protein *44 g*;
Carbohydrate *9 g*; Fat *21 g*; Saturates *8 g*

✪✪✪ moderate
  30 mins
🕐 45 mins

Served in scallop shells, this unusual chicken dish makes a stylish presentation for an appetizer or a light lunch.

Chicken Scallops

SERVES 4

1 ½ cups short-cut macaroni, or other short pasta shapes
3 tbsp vegetable oil, plus extra for brushing
1 onion, finely chopped
3 slices unsmoked Canadian bacon, rind removed, chopped
2 cups button mushrooms, sliced thinly or chopped
6 oz/175 g cooked chicken, diced
¾ cup unsweetened yogurt
4 tbsp dry bread crumbs
½ cup grated sharp colby cheese
salt and pepper
flatleaf parsley sprigs, to garnish

1 Cook the pasta in a large pan of boiling salted water with 1 tablespoon of oil for 8–10 minutes. Drain the pasta, return to the pan, and cover.

2 Heat the broiler to medium. Heat the remaining oil in a skillet over medium heat and pan-fry the onion until translucent. Add the bacon and mushrooms and cook for 3–4 minutes, stirring once or twice.

3 Stir in the pasta, chicken, and yogurt and season to taste with salt and pepper.

4 Brush four large scallop shells with oil. Spoon in the chicken mixture and smooth to make neat mounds.

5 Mix together the bread crumbs and cheese, and sprinkle over the top of the shells. Press the topping lightly into the chicken mixture, and broil for 4–5 minutes, until golden brown and bubbling. Garnish with flatleaf parsley sprigs, and serve hot.

NUTRITION
Calories 532; Sugars 3 g; Protein 25 g;
Carbohydrate 33 g; Fat 34 g; Saturates 14 g

moderate

20 mins

25 mins

A rich caramelized sauce, flavored with balsamic vinegar and wine, gives this chicken dish a piquant flavor. Serve with polenta or rice.

Chicken *with* Balsamic Vinegar

1 Using a sharp knife, make a few slashes in the skin of the chicken. Brush the chicken with the minced garlic and place in a nonmetallic dish.

2 Pour the wine and white wine vinegar over the chicken and season. Cover and leave to marinate in the refrigerator overnight.

3 Remove the chicken pieces with a draining spoon, draining well, and reserve the marinade.

4 Heat the oil and butter in a skillet. Add the shallots and cook for 2–3 minutes, or until they begin to soften.

5 Add the chicken pieces to the skillet and cook for 3–4 minutes, turning, until browned all over. Reduce the heat and add half of the reserved marinade. Cover and cook for 15–20 minutes, adding more marinade when necessary.

6 Once the chicken is tender, add the balsamic vinegar and thyme and cook for an additional 4 minutes.

7 Transfer the chicken and marinade to serving plates and serve.

SERVES 4

4 chicken thighs, boned
2 garlic cloves, minced
¾ cup red wine
3 tbsp white wine vinegar
1 tbsp oil
1 tbsp butter
4 shallots
3 tbsp balsamic vinegar
2 tbsp chopped fresh thyme
salt and pepper
cooked polenta or rice, to serve

NUTRITION
Calories *148*; Sugars *0.2 g*; Protein *11 g*; Carbohydrate *0.2 g*; Fat *8 g*; Saturates *3 g*

 easy

8 hrs 10 mins

35 mins

COOK'S TIP

To make the chicken pieces look a little neater, use wooden skewers or toothpicks to hold them together or secure them with a length of string.

Olives are a popular flavoring for poultry and game in the Apulia region of Italy, where this recipe originates.

Chicken *with* Green Olives

SERVES 4

3 tbsp olive oil

2 tbsp butter

4 chicken breasts, part boned

1 large onion, chopped finely

2 garlic cloves, minced

2 red, yellow, or green bell peppers, halved, seeded, and cut into large pieces

4 cups sliced white mushrooms

2 tomatoes, skinned and halved

⅝ cup dry white wine

1½ cups pitted green olives

4–6 tbsp heavy cream

14 oz/400 g dried pasta

salt and pepper

chopped flatleaf parsley, to garnish

NUTRITION
Calories *614*; Sugars *6 g*; Protein *34 g*;
Carbohydrate *49 g*; Fat *30 g*; Saturates *11 g*

✪✪✪   moderate

◔   15 mins

◷   1 hr 30 mins

1 Heat 2 tablespoons of the oil and the butter in a skillet. Add the chicken breasts and cook until golden brown all over, then remove from the skillet.

2 Add the onion and garlic to the skillet and cook over a medium heat until beginning to soften. Add the bell peppers and mushrooms and cook for 2–3 minutes. Add the tomatoes and season to taste with salt and pepper. Transfer the vegetables to a casserole and arrange the chicken on top.

3 Add the wine to the pan and bring to a boil. Pour the wine over the chicken. Cover and cook in a preheated oven, at 350°F/180°C, for 50 minutes.

4 Add the olives to the casserole and mix in. Pour in the cream, then cover and return to the oven for an additional 10–20 minutes.

5 Meanwhile, bring a large pan of lightly salted water to a boil. Add the pasta and the remaining oil and cook until tender, but still firm to the bite. Drain the pasta and transfer to a serving dish.

6 Arrange the chicken on top of the pasta, then spoon over the sauce and garnish with the parsley, and serve immediately. Alternatively, place the pasta in a large serving bowl and serve separately.

This Italian-style dish is richly flavored with pesto, which is a mixture of basil, olive oil, pinenuts, and Parmesan cheese. Either red or green pesto can be used for this recipe.

Broiled Chicken *with* Pesto Toasts

1 Arrange the chicken in a single layer in a wide flameproof dish and brush lightly with oil. Place under a preheated broiler for about 15 minutes, turning occasionally until golden brown.

2 Pierce with a skewer to ensure that the chicken is cooked and there is no trace of pink in the chicken juices.

3 Pour off any excess fat. Warm the crushed tomatoes and half the pesto sauce in a small pan and pour over the chicken. Broil for a few more minutes, turning until coated.

4 Meanwhile, spread the remaining pesto on to the slices of bread. Arrange the bread over the chicken and sprinkle with the Parmesan cheese. Scatter the pinenuts over the cheese. Broil for 2–3 minutes, or until browned and bubbling. Serve hot, garnished with a fresh basil sprig.

SERVES 4

8 chicken thighs, part boned
olive oil, for brushing
1²/₃ cups crushed tomatoes
2 quantities of Pesto Sauce (see page 133)
12 slices French bread
1 cup freshly grated Parmesan cheese
¹/₂ cup pinenuts or slivered almonds
fresh basil sprig, to garnish

NUTRITION
Calories *787*; Sugars *6 g*; Protein *45 g*;
Carbohydrate *70 g*; Fat *38 g*; Saturates *9 g*

⭐⭐	easy
🕐	10 mins
🕐	25 mins

🍳 COOK'S TIP

Leaving the skin on means the chicken will have a higher fat content, but many people like the rich taste and crispy skin, especially when it is blackened on the broiler. The skin also keeps in the cooking juices.

You need to put in a bit of effort to prepare the chicken, but once marinated it's an easy and tasty candidate for the barbecue grill.

Chargrilled Chicken

SERVES 4

3½ lb/1.5 kg whole chicken
grated rind of 1 lemon
4 tbsp lemon juice
2 fresh rosemary sprigs
1 small fresh red chile, chopped finely
⅔ cup olive oil

1 Split the chicken down the breast bone and open it out. Trim off excess fat, and remove the parson's nose, wing, and leg tips. Break the leg and wing joints to enable you to pound it flat. This ensures that it cooks evenly. Cover the split chicken with plastic wrap and pound it as flat as possible with a rolling pin.

2 Mix the lemon rind and juice, rosemary sprigs, chile and olive oil together in a small bowl. Place the chicken in a large dish and pour over the marinade, turning the chicken to coat it evenly. Cover the dish and leave the chicken to marinate for at least 2 hours in the refrigerator.

3 Cook the chicken over a hot barbecue grill (the coals should be white, and red when fanned) for about 30 minutes, turning it regularly until the skin is golden and crisp. To test if it is cooked, pierce one of the chicken thighs; the juices will run clear, not pink, when it is ready. Serve.

NUTRITION
Calories *129*; Sugars *0 g*; Protein *22 g*;
Carbohydrate *0 g*; Fat *5 g*; Saturates *1 g*

moderate

2 hrs 30 mins

30 mins

Chicken pieces are cooked in a succulent, lemon and mild mustard sauce, then coated in poppy seeds and served on a bed of fresh pasta shells.

Lemon Chicken Conchiglie

1 Arrange the chicken pieces, smooth side down, in a single layer in a large ovenproof dish.

2 Mix together the butter, mustard, lemon juice, sugar, and paprika in a bowl and season to taste with salt and pepper. Brush the mixture over the upper surfaces of the chicken pieces and bake in a preheated oven, 400°F/200°C, for 15 minutes.

3 Remove the dish from the oven and carefully turn over the chicken pieces. Coat the upper surfaces of the chicken with the remaining mustard mixture, then sprinkle the chicken pieces with poppy seeds and return to the oven for an additional 15 minutes.

4 Meanwhile, bring a large pan of lightly salted water to a boil. Add the pasta shells and olive oil and cook until tender, but still firm to the bite.

5 Drain the pasta and arrange on a warmed serving dish. Top with the chicken, pour over the sauce and serve immediately.

SERVES 4

8 chicken pieces, each about 4 oz
4 tbsp butter, melted
4 tbsp mild mustard (see Cook's Tip)
2 tbsp lemon juice
1 tbsp brown sugar
1 tsp paprika
3 tbsp poppy seeds
14 oz/400 g fresh pasta shells
1 tbsp olive oil
salt and pepper

NUTRITION
Calories *652*; Sugars *5 g*; Protein *51 g*;
Carbohydrate *46 g*; Fat *31 g*; Saturates *12 g*

 COOK'S TIP

Dijon is the type of mustard most often used in cooking, because it has a clean and mildly spicy flavor. German mustard has a sweet-sour taste, with Bavarian mustard being slightly sweeter. American mustard is mild and sweet.

easy
10 mins
35 mins

Napoleon's chef was ordered to cook a sumptuous meal on the eve of the battle of Marengo. He gathered everything possible to make a feast, and this was the result.

Chicken Marengo

SERVES 4

8 chicken pieces
1 tbsp olive oil
1 cup tomato paste
¾ cup white wine
2 tsp dried mixed herbs
1½ oz butter, melted
2 garlic cloves, crushed
8 slices white bread
1 ½ cups sliced mixed mushrooms (such as white, oyster, and ceps)
16–18 pitted black olives, chopped
1 tsp sugar
fresh basil, to garnish

1 Using a sharp knife, remove the bone from each of the chicken pieces.

2 Heat the oil in a large skillet. Add the chicken pieces and cook for 4–5 minutes, turning occasionally, or until browned all over.

3 Add the tomato paste, wine, and mixed herbs to the skillet. Bring to a boil and then simmer for 30 minutes or until the chicken is tender and the juices run clear when a skewer is inserted into the thickest part of the meat.

4 To make the bruschetta, mix the melted butter and crushed garlic together. Lightly toast the slices of bread and brush with the garlic butter.

5 Add the remaining oil to a separate skillet and cook the mushrooms for 2–3 minutes or until just brown.

6 Add the olives and sugar to the chicken mixture and warm through.

7 Transfer the chicken and sauce to serving plates. Garnish with basil. Serve with the bruschetta and cooked mushrooms.

NUTRITION
Calories *521*; Sugars *6 g*; Protein *47 g*;
Carbohydrate *34 g*; Fat *19 g*; Saturates *8 g*

moderate

20 mins

50 mins

🎩 **COOK'S TIP**

You can use any sort of Italian bread, such as ciabatta, to make the bruschetta, or slices of French bread.

A raspberry and honey sauce superbly counterbalances the richness of the duck.

Duck *with* Raspberry Sauce

1 Trim and score the duck breasts with a sharp knife and season well all over. Melt the butter in a skillet, then add the duck breasts and cook until lightly colored on all sides.

2 Add the carrots, shallots, lemon juice, and half the meat bouillon and simmer over a low heat for 1 minute. Stir in half the honey and half the raspberries. Sprinkle over half the flour and cook, stirring constantly for 3 minutes. Season with pepper and add the Worcestershire sauce.

3 Stir in the remaining bouillon and cook for 1 minute. Stir in the remaining honey and remaining raspberries and sprinkle over the remaining flour. Cook for a further 3 minutes.

4 Remove the duck breasts from the pan, but leave the sauce to continue simmering over a very low heat, stirring occasionally.

5 Meanwhile, bring a large pan of lightly salted water to a boil. Add the linguine and olive oil and cook until tender, but still firm to the bite. Drain and divide between 4 individual plates.

6 Slice the duck breast lengthwise into ¼-inch/5-mm thick pieces. Pour a little sauce over the pasta and arrange the sliced duck in a fan shape on top of it. Garnish with raspberries and flatleaf parsley and serve.

SERVES 4

4 boned breasts of duck, about 10 oz/285 g each
2 tbsp butter
⅜ cup finely chopped carrots
4 tbsp finely chopped shallots
1 tbsp lemon juice
⅝ cup meat bouillon
4 tbsp clear honey
¾ cup fresh or frozen raspberries, thawed if frozen
¼ cup all-purpose flour
1 tbsp Worcestershire sauce
14 oz/400 g fresh linguine
1 tbsp olive oil
salt and pepper

to garnish
fresh raspberries
fresh flatleaf parsley sprig

NUTRITION
Calories *686*; Sugars *15 g*; Protein *62 g*; Carbohydrate *70 g*; Fat *20 g*; Saturates *7 g*

⭐⭐⭐   moderate
🕐   15 mins
🕐   25 mins

This scrumptious and unusual baked lasagna is virtually a meal in itself.

Pheasant Lasagna

SERVES 4

butter, for greasing
14 sheets precooked lasagna
3¾ cups Béchamel Sauce (see page 14)
¾ cup grated mozzarella cheese

filling

8 oz/225 g pork fat, diced
2 tbsp butter
16 small onions
8 large pheasant breasts, sliced thinly
¼ cup all-purpose flour
2½ cups chicken bouillon
1 bouquet garni
1 lb/450 g fresh English peas, shelled
salt and pepper

NUTRITION

Calories *1038*; Sugars *13 g*; Protein *65 g*;
Carbohydrate *54 g*; Fat *64 g*; Saturates *27 g*

 challenging

20 mins

1 hr 15 mins

1 To make the filling, put the pork fat into a pan of boiling, salted water and simmer for 3 minutes, then drain and pat dry.

2 Melt the butter in a large skillet. Add the pork fat and onions and cook for 3 minutes, or until lightly browned.

3 Remove the pork fat and onions from the pan and set aside. Add the slices of pheasant and cook over a low heat for 12 minutes, or until browned all over. Transfer to an ovenproof dish.

4 Stir the flour into the pan and cook until just brown, then blend in the bouillon. Pour over the pheasant and add the bouquet garni, then cook in a preheated oven, 400°F/200°C, for 5 minutes.

5 Remove the bouquet garni. Add the onions, pork fat, and peas and return to the oven for 10 minutes.

6 Put the pheasant and pork fat in a food processor and grind finely.

7 Lower the oven temperature to 375°F/190°C. Lightly grease an ovenproof dish with butter. Build layers of lasagna, ground pheasant, and Béchamel Sauce in the dish, ending with Béchamel Sauce. Sprinkle over the cheese and bake in the oven for 30 minutes. Serve surrounded by the peas and onions.

Partridge has a more delicate flavor than many game birds and this subtle sauce perfectly complements it.

Lime Partridge *with* Pesto

1 Arrange the partridge pieces, smooth-side down, in a single layer in a large, ovenproof dish.

2 Mix together the butter, Dijon mustard, lime juice, and brown sugar in a bowl. Season to taste with salt and pepper. Brush this mixture over the uppermost surfaces of the partridge pieces and bake in a preheated oven, 400°F/200°C, for 15 minutes.

3 Remove the dish from the oven and coat the partridge pieces with 3 tablespoons of the Pesto Sauce. Return to the oven and bake for an additional 12 minutes.

4 Remove the dish from the oven and carefully turn over the partridge pieces. Coat the top of the partridges with the remaining mustard mixture and return to the oven for an additional 10 minutes.

5 Meanwhile, bring a large pan of lightly salted water to a boil. Add the rigatoni and olive oil and cook for about 10 minutes, or until tender, but still firm to the bite. Drain and transfer to a large serving dish. Toss the pasta with the remaining Pesto Sauce and the Parmesan cheese.

6 Arrange the pieces of partridge on the serving dish with the rigatoni, then pour over the cooking juices and serve immediately.

SERVES 4

8 partridge pieces (about 4 oz/115 g each)
4 tbsp butter, melted
4 tbsp Dijon mustard
2 tbsp lime juice
1 tbsp brown sugar
6 tbsp Pesto Sauce (see page 133)
1 lb/450 g dried rigatoni
1 tbsp olive oil
1⅓ cups freshly grated Parmesan cheese
salt and pepper

NUTRITION
Calories *895*; Sugars *5 g*; Protein *79 g*;
Carbohydrate *45 g*; Fat *45 g*; Saturates *18 g*

 challenging

15 mins

40 mins

Pasta

The simplicity and satisfying nature of pasta in all its varieties makes it a universal favorite. Easy to cook and economical, pasta is wonderfully versatile. It can be served with sauces made from meat, fish, or vegetables, or baked in the oven. The classic Spaghetti Bolognese needs no introduction, and yet it is said that there are almost as many versions of this delicious regional dish as there are lovers of Italian food! Fish and seafood are irresistible combined with pasta and need only the briefest of cooking times. Pasta combined with vegetables provides inspiration for countless dishes which will please vegetarians and meat-eaters alike. The delicious pasta dishes in this chapter range from easy, economic mid-week suppers to sophisticated and elegant meals for special occasions.

The original recipe takes about 4 hours to cook and should be left overnight to allow the flavors to mingle. This version is much quicker.

Spaghetti Bolognese

SERVES 4

1 tbsp olive oil
1 onion, finely chopped
2 garlic cloves, chopped
1 carrot, scraped and chopped
1 celery stick, chopped
½ cup pancetta or streaky bacon, diced
12 oz/350 g lean ground beef
2 cups chopped tomatoes
2 tsp dried oregano
scant ½ cup red wine
2 tbsp tomato paste
salt and pepper
1 ½ lb/675 g fresh spaghetti or 12 oz/350 g dried spaghetti

1 Heat the oil in a large skillet. Add the onions and cook for 3 minutes.

2 Add the garlic, carrot, celery, and pancetta or bacon and sauté for 3–4 minutes or until just beginning to brown.

3 Add the beef and cook over a high heat for another 3 minutes or until all of the meat is brown.

4 Stir in the tomatoes, oregano, and red wine and bring to a boil. Reduce the heat and leave to simmer for about 45 minutes.

5 Stir in the tomato paste and season with salt and pepper.

6 Cook the spaghetti in a pan of salted boiling water for 8–10 minutes until tender, but still has "bite." Drain thoroughly.

7 Transfer the spaghetti to a serving plate and pour over the bolognese sauce. Toss to mix well and serve hot.

NUTRITION
Calories *591*; Sugars *7 g*; Protein *29 g*;
Carbohydrate *640 g*; Fat *24 g*; Saturates *9 g*

 easy
20 mins
1 hr 5 mins

 **COOK'S TIP**

Try adding 1 oz/25 g dried porcini, soaked for 10 minutes in 2 tablespoons of warm water, to the Bolognese sauce in step 4, if you wish.

Lightly cooked eggs and pancetta are combined with cheese to make this rich, classic sauce.

Pasta Carbonara

1 Heat the oil and butter in a skillet until the butter is just beginning to froth.

2 Add the pancetta or bacon to the pan and cook for 5 minutes or until browned all over.

3 Mix together the eggs and milk in a small bowl. Stir in the thyme and season to taste with salt and pepper.

4 Cook the pasta in a pan of salted boiling water for 8–10 minutes until tender, but still has "bite." Drain thoroughly.

5 Add the cooked, drained pasta to the skillet with the eggs and cook over a high heat for about 30 seconds or until the eggs just begin to cook and set. Do not overcook the eggs or they will become rubbery.

6 Add half of the grated Parmesan cheese, stirring to combine.

7 Transfer the pasta to a serving plate, pour over the sauce and toss to mix well together.

8 Sprinkle the rest of the grated Parmesan over the top and serve.

SERVES 4

1 tbsp olive oil
3 tbsp butter
¾ cup diced pancetta or unsmoked bacon
3 eggs, beaten
2 tbsp milk
1 tbsp fresh thyme leaves
1½ lb/675 g fresh or 12 oz/350 g dried conchiglioni rigati
½ cup grated Parmesan cheese
salt and pepper

NUTRITION
Calories *547*; Sugars *1 g*; Protein *21 g*;
Carbohydrate *49 g*; Fat *31 g*; Saturates *14 g*

easy

 15 mins

 20 mins

Fresh tomatoes make a delicious Italian-style sauce which goes particularly well with pasta.

Italian Tomato Sauce *and* Pasta

SERVES 2

1 tbsp olive oil

1 small onion, chopped finely

1–2 garlic cloves, crushed

4 tomatoes, peeled and chopped

2 tsp tomato paste

2 tbsp water

3–4 dried pasta shapes

¾ cup lean bacon, de-rinded and diced

½ cup mushrooms, sliced

1 tbsp chopped fresh parsley or 1 tsp chopped fresh cilantro

2 tbsp sour cream or natural fromage frais (optional)

salt and pepper

1 To make the tomato sauce, heat the oil in a pan and cook the onion and garlic gently, until soft.

2 Add the tomatoes, tomato paste, water, and salt and pepper to the mixture in the pan and bring to the boil. Cover and simmer gently for 10 minutes.

3 Meanwhile, cook the pasta in a pan of salted boiling water for 8–10 minutes, or until just tender. Drain the pasta thoroughly and transfer to warm serving dishes.

4 Heat the bacon gently in a skillet until the fat runs, then add the mushrooms and continue cooking for 3–4 minutes. Drain off any excess oil.

5 Add the bacon and mushrooms to the tomato mixture, together with the parsley and the sour cream, if using. Reheat and serve with the pasta.

NUTRITION

Calories *304*; Sugars *8 g*; Protein *15 g*; Carbohydrate *31 g*; Fat *14 g*; Saturates *5 g*

⭐ very easy

🕐 10 mins

🕐 25 mins

  **COOK'S TIP**

Choose any variety of pasta shape for this dish, although pasta tubes and shells are the best for holding the sauce.

The different shapes and textures of the vegetables make a mouthwatering presentation in this light and summery dish.

Broccoli *and* Asparagus Gemelli

1 Bring a large pan of lightly salted water to a boil. Add the pasta and olive oil and cook until tender, but still firm to the bite. Drain and return to the pan, then cover and keep warm.

2 Steam the broccoli, zucchini, asparagus spears, and snow peas over a pan of boiling salted water until they are just beginning to soften. Remove from the heat and refresh in cold water. Drain and set aside.

3 Bring a small pan of lightly salted water to a boil. Add the frozen peas and cook for 3 minutes. Drain the peas and refresh in cold water then drain again. Set aside with the other vegetables.

4 Put the butter and vegetable bouillon in a pan over a medium heat. Add all of the vegetables, reserving a few of the asparagus spears, then toss carefully with a wooden spoon until they have heated through, taking care not to break them up.

5 Stir in the cream and heat through, without bringing to a boil. Season to taste with salt, pepper, and nutmeg.

6 Transfer the pasta to a warmed serving dish and stir in the chopped parsley. Spoon over the vegetable sauce and sprinkle over the Parmesan cheese. Arrange the reserved asparagus spears in a pattern on top and serve.

SERVES 4

2 cups dried gemelli or other pasta shapes
1 tbsp olive oil
1 head green broccoli, cut into flowerets
2 zucchini, sliced
8 oz/225 g asparagus spears
1 ½ cups snow peas
1 cup frozen peas
2 tbsp butter
3 tbsp vegetable bouillon
4 tbsp heavy cream
freshly grated nutmeg
2 tbsp chopped fresh parsley
2 tbsp freshly grated Parmesan cheese
salt and pepper

NUTRITION
Calories 517; Sugars 5 g; Protein 17 g;
Carbohydrate 42 g; Fat 32 g; Saturates 18 g

easy

10 mins

25 mins

A Mediterranean mixture of red bell peppers, garlic, and zucchini, cooked in olive oil and tossed with pasta spirals.

Pasta *and* Vegetable Sauce

SERVES 4

3 tbsp olive oil
1 onion, sliced
2 garlic cloves, chopped
3 red bell peppers, halved, seeded and cut into strips
3 zucchini, sliced
2 cups canned chopped tomatoes
3 tbsp sun-dried tomato paste
2 tbsp chopped fresh basil
8 oz/225 g fresh fusilli
1 cup grated Swiss cheese
salt and pepper
fresh basil sprigs, to garnish

1 Heat the oil in a heavy-based pan or flameproof casserole. Add the onion and garlic and cook, stirring occasionally, until softened. Add the bell peppers and zucchini and cook, stirring occasionally, for 5 minutes.

2 Add the tomatoes, sun-dried tomato paste, and basil, and season to taste with salt and pepper. Cover and cook for a further 5 minutes.

3 Meanwhile, bring a large pan of salted water to a boil and add the pasta. Stir and bring back to a boil. Reduce the heat slightly and cook, uncovered, for 3 minutes, until just tender. Drain the pasta thoroughly and add to the vegetable mixture. Toss gently to mix well.

4 Transfer to a shallow flameproof dish and sprinkle with the cheese.

5 Cook under a preheated broiler for 5 minutes, until the cheese is golden brown and bubbling. Garnish with basil sprigs and serve immediately.

NUTRITION
Calories *341*; Sugars *8 g*; Protein *13 g*;
Carbohydrate *30 g*; Fat *20 g*; Saturates *8 g*

very easy

15 mins

20 mins

Delicious stirred into pasta, soups, and salad dressings, pesto is available in most supermarkets, but making your own gives a much fresher, fuller flavor.

Pasta *with* Classic Pesto Sauce

1 Rinse the basil leaves and pat them dry with paper towels.

2 Put the basil leaves, garlic, pinenuts, and Parmesan cheese into a food processor and blend for about 30 seconds, or until smooth. Alternatively, pound the ingredients by hand, using a mortar and pestle.

3 If you are using a food processor, keep the motor running and slowly add the olive oil. Alternatively, add the oil drop by drop while stirring briskly. Season with salt and pepper.

4 Meanwhile, cook the pasta in a pan of salted boiling water according to the pack instructions, or until it is cooked through, but still has bite. Drain.

5 Transfer the pasta to a serving plate and serve with the pesto. Toss to mix well and serve hot.

SERVES 4

about 40 fresh basil leaves, washed and dried
3 garlic cloves, minced
¼ cup pinenuts
½ cup finely grated Parmesan cheese
3 tbsp extra-virgin olive oil
salt and pepper
1½ lb/675 g fresh pasta or 12 oz/350 g dried pasta

NUTRITION
Calories 321; Sugars 1 g; Protein 11 g; Carbohydrate 32 g; Fat 17 g; Saturates 4 g

 very easy
 15 mins
 10 mins

🍴 **COOK'S TIP**

You can store pesto in the refrigerator for about 4 weeks. Cover the surface of the pesto with olive oil before sealing the container or bottle, to prevent the basil from oxidizing and turning black.

A deliciously fresh and slightly spicy tomato sauce which is excellent for lunch or a light supper.

Chile Tagliatelle

SERVES 4

3 tbsp butter
1 onion, chopped finely
1 garlic clove, minced
2 small fresh red chiles, seeded and diced
1 lb/450 g fresh tomatoes, peeled, seeded, and diced
¾ cup vegetable bouillon
2 tbsp tomato paste
1 tsp sugar
salt and pepper
1½ lb/675 g fresh green and white tagliatelle, or 12 oz/350 g dried

1 Melt the butter in a large pan. Add the onion and garlic and cook for 3–4 minutes, or until softened.

2 Add the chiles to the pan and continue cooking for about 2 minutes more.

3 Add the tomatoes and bouillon, then reduce the heat and let simmer for 10 minutes, stirring.

4 Pour the sauce into a food processor and blend for 1 minute, or until smooth. Alternatively, push the sauce through a strainer.

5 Return the sauce to the pan and add the tomato paste, sugar, and salt and pepper to taste. Gently reheat over a low heat, until piping hot.

6 Cook the tagliatelle in a pan of boiling water according to the pack instructions or until it is cooked, but still has bite. Drain the tagliatelle and transfer to serving plates. Serve with the tomato sauce.

NUTRITION
Calories *306*; Sugars *7 g*; Protein *8 g*;
Carbohydrate *45 g*; Fat *12 g*; Saturates *7 g*

⭐⭐ easy
🖐 15 mins
🕐 35 mins

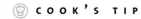

🍳 **COOK'S TIP**

Try topping your pasta dish with ½ cup pancetta or unsmoked bacon, diced and dry-fried for 5 minutes, or until crispy.

A satisfying winter dish, this pasta and bean casserole with a crunchy topping is a slow-cooked, one-pot meal.

Casseroled Beans *and* Penne

1 Put the navy beans in a large pan and add sufficient cold water to cover. Bring to a boil and continue to boil vigorously for 20 minutes. Drain, set aside, and keep warm.

2 Bring a large pan of lightly salted water to a boil. Add the penne and 1 tablespoon of the olive oil and cook for about 3 minutes. Drain the pasta. Set aside and keep warm.

3 Put the beans in a large, flameproof casserole. Add the vegetable bouillon and stir in the remaining olive oil, the onions, garlic, bay leaves, oregano, thyme, wine, and tomato paste. Bring to a boil, then cover and cook in a heated oven, at 350°F/180°C, for 2 hours.

4 Add the penne, celery, fennel, mushrooms, and tomatoes to the casserole and season to taste with salt and pepper. Stir in the muscovado sugar and sprinkle over the bread crumbs. Cover and cook in the oven for 1 more hour.

5 Serve hot with salad greens and crusty bread.

SERVES 4

1¼ cups dried navy beans, soaked overnight and drained
2 cups dried penne
6 tbsp olive oil
3½ cups vegetable bouillon
2 large onions, sliced
2 garlic cloves, chopped
2 bay leaves
1 tsp dried oregano
1 tsp dried thyme
5 tbsp red wine
2 tbsp tomato paste
2 celery stalks, sliced
1 fennel bulb, sliced
1⅝ cups sliced mushrooms
3 tomatoes, sliced
1 tsp dark muscovado sugar
4 tbsp dry white bread crumbs
salt and pepper

to serve
salad greens
crusty bread

NUTRITION
Calories 323; Sugars 5 g; Protein 13 g; Carbohydrate 41 g; Fat 12 g; Saturates 2 g

 moderate
8 hrs 25 mins
3 hrs 30 mins

The tasty flavors and delightful textures of artichoke hearts and black olives make a winning combination.

Artichoke *and* Olive Spaghetti

SERVES 4

2 tbsp olive oil
1 large red onion, chopped
2 garlic cloves, crushed
1 tbsp lemon juice
4 baby eggplants, quartered
2½ cups crushed tomatoes
2 tsp superfine sugar
2 tbsp tomato paste
14 oz/400 g canned artichoke hearts, drained and halved
1 cup pitted black olives
12 oz/350 g whole-wheat dried spaghetti
salt and pepper
fresh basil sprigs, to garnish
olive bread, to serve

1 Heat 1 tablespoon of the oil in a large, heavy skillet. Add the onion, garlic, lemon juice, and eggplants and cook over low heat, stirring occasionally, for 4–5 minutes or until lightly browned.

2 Pour in the crushed tomatoes, season with salt and pepper to taste, and stir in the sugar and tomato paste. Bring to a boil, reduce the heat and simmer gently for 20 minutes.

3 Gently stir in the artichoke hearts and olives and cook for 5 minutes.

4 Meanwhile, bring a large pan of lightly salted water to a boil. Add the pasta, bring back to a boil, and cook for 8–10 minutes or until tender, but still firm to the bite. Drain, toss in the remaining oil, and season to taste.

5 Transfer the spaghetti to a warmed serving bowl and top with the vegetable sauce. Garnish with basil sprigs and serve with olive bread.

NUTRITION
Calories *393*; Sugars *11 g*; Protein *14 g*; Carbohydrate *63 g*; Fat *11 g*; Saturates *2 g*

easy

20 mins

35 mins

 **COOK'S TIP**

Instead of spaghetti you could use any long pasta, such as tagliatelle, pappardelle or fettuccine.

This roasted pepper and chile pasta sauce is sweet and spicy.

Fusilli Salad *with* Chile

1 Place the bell peppers, skin-side up, on a cookie sheet with the chile and garlic. Cook under a preheated broiler for 15 minutes, or until charred. After 10 minutes, add the tomatoes and broil skin-side up.

2 Place the bell peppers and chile in a plastic bag and let them sweat for 10 minutes.

3 Remove the skin from the bell peppers and chile and slice the flesh into strips, using a sharp knife.

4 Peel the garlic and peel and seed the tomatoes.

5 Place the chopped almonds on a cookie sheet and place under the broiler for 2–3 minutes, or until golden.

6 Using a food processor, blend the bell pepper, chile, garlic, and tomatoes to make a paste. Keep the motor running and slowly add the olive oil to form a thick sauce. Alternatively, mash the mixture with a fork and beat in the olive oil, drop by drop.

7 Stir the chopped almonds into the mixture.

8 Warm the sauce in a pan until it is heated through.

9 Cook the pasta in a pan of salted boiling water according to the pack instructions, or until it is cooked through, but still has bite. Drain the pasta and transfer to a serving dish. Pour over the sauce and toss to mix. Garnish with fresh oregano leaves.

SERVES 4

2 red bell peppers, halved and seeded
1 small fresh red chile
2 garlic cloves
4 tomatoes, halved
²⁄₃ cup chopped almonds
100 ml/3 ½ fl oz olive oil
1 lb 8 oz/675 g fresh pasta or 12 oz/350 g dried pasta
fresh oregano leaves, to garnish

NUTRITION
Calories *423*; Sugars *5 g*; Protein *9 g*; Carbohydrate *38 g*; Fat *27 g*; Saturates *4 g*

⚝⚝⚝ moderate

🕐 25 mins

🕐 30 mins

This pasta dish can be prepared in a moment—the intense flavors are sure to make this a popular recipe.

Tagliatelle *and* Garlic Sauce

SERVES 4

2 tbsp walnut oil
1 bunch scallions, sliced
2 garlic cloves, thinly sliced
4 cups sliced mushrooms
1 lb/450 g fresh green and white tagliatelle
8 oz/225 g frozen chopped leaf spinach, thawed and drained
½ cup full-fat soft cheese with garlic and herbs
4 tbsp light cream
½ cup chopped, unsalted pistachio nuts
2 tbsp shredded fresh basil
salt and pepper
sprigs of fresh basil, to garnish
Italian bread, to serve

1 Gently heat the oil in a wok or skillet and pan-fry the scallions and garlic for 1 minute or until just softened. Add the mushrooms, stir well, cover and cook gently for 5 minutes or until softened.

2 Meanwhile, bring a large pan of lightly salted water to the boil and cook the pasta for 3–5 minutes or until just tender. Drain the pasta thoroughly and return to the pan.

3 Add the spinach to the mushrooms and heat through for 1–2 minutes. Add the cheese and allow to melt slightly. Stir in the cream and continue to heat without allowing to boil.

4 Pour the mixture over the pasta, season to taste and mix well. Heat gently, stirring, for 2–3 minutes.

5 Pile into a warmed serving bowl and sprinkle over the pistachio nuts and shredded basil. Garnish with basil sprigs and serve with Italian bread.

NUTRITION
Calories *501*; Sugars *3 g*; Protein *15 g*;
Carbohydrate *43 g*; Fat *31 g*; Saturates *11 g*

very easy

15 mins

20 mins

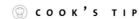 **COOK'S TIP**

Be sure to drain the spinach well before adding to the recipe.

Layers of cheese sauce, smoked cod and wholewheat lasagna can be assembled overnight and left ready to cook on the following day.

Fish *and* Vegetable Lasagna

1 Cook the lasagna in a pan of boiling, salted water until almost tender. Drain and reserve.

2 Place the smoked cod, milk, lemon juice, peppercorns, bay leaves, and parsley stalks in a skillet. Bring to a boil, cover and simmer for 10 minutes.

3 Lift the fish from the pan with a draining spoon. Remove the skin and any bones. Flake the fish. Strain and reserve the liquor.

4 To make the sauce, melt the butter in a pan and cook the onion, bell pepper and zucchini for 2–3 minutes. Stir in the flour and cook for 1 minute. Gradually add the fish liquor, the wine, cream, and shrimp. Simmer for 2 minutes. Remove from the heat, add the cheese, and season.

5 Grease a shallow baking dish. Pour in a quarter of the sauce and spread evenly over the base. Cover the sauce with three sheets of lasagna, then with another quarter of the sauce.

6 Arrange the fish on top, then cover with half of the remaining sauce. Finish with the remaining lasagna, then the rest of the sauce. Sprinkle the colby cheese and Parmesan over the sauce.

7 Bake in a preheated oven, 375°F/190°C, for 25 minutes, or until the top is golden brown and bubbling. Garnish and serve.

SERVES 6

8 sheets wholewheat lasagna
1 lb/450 g smoked cod
2½ cups milk
1 tbsp lemon juice
8 peppercorns
2 bay leaves
a few fresh parsley stalks
½ cup grated sharp colby cheese
¼ cup grated Parmesan cheese
salt and pepper
a few whole shrimp, to garnish

sauce

¼ cup butter, plus extra for greasing
1 large onion, sliced
1 green bell pepper, halved, seeded, and chopped
1 small zucchini, sliced
½ cup all-purpose flour
⅔ cup white wine
⅔ cup light cream
4½ oz/125 g shelled shrimp
½ cup grated sharp colby cheese

NUTRITION

Calories *456*; Sugars *8 g*; Protein *33 g*; Carbohydrate *24 g*; Fat *24 g*; Saturates *15 g*

⚝⚝⚝   moderate

    25 mins

🕐   50 mins

The pappardelle and vegetables are tossed in a delicious chili and tomato sauce for a quick and economical meal.

Pasta *and* Chili Tomatoes

SERVES 4

10 oz/280 g dried pappardelle
3 tbsp peanut oil
2 garlic cloves, crushed
2 shallots, sliced
2¼ cups sliced dwarf beans
8 cherry tomatoes, halved
1 tsp chili flakes
4 tbsp crunchy peanut butter
⅔ cup coconut milk
1 tbsp tomato paste
sliced scallions, to garnish

1 Bring a large pan of lightly salted water to a boil. Add the pappardelle, bring back to a boil, and cook for 8–10 minutes until tender, but still firm to the bite. Drain thoroughly and set aside.

2 Meanwhile, heat the peanut oil in a large, heavy skillet or preheated wok. Add the garlic and shallots and stir-fry for 1 minute.

3 Add the green beans and drained pasta to the skillet or wok and stir-fry for 5 minutes. Add the cherry tomatoes and mix well.

4 Combine the chili flakes, peanut butter, coconut milk, and tomato paste in a bowl. Pour the chili mixture into the skillet or wok, toss well to combine, and heat through.

5 Transfer to warm serving dishes and garnish with scallion slices. Serve immediately.

NUTRITION

Calories *353*; Sugars *7 g*; Protein 10 *g*;
Carbohydrate *26 g*; Fat *24 g*; Saturates *4 g*

very easy

15 mins

20 mins

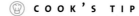 COOK'S TIP

Add slices of chicken or beef to the recipe and stir-fry with the beans and pasta in step 3 for a more substantial main meal.

Frozen shelled shrimp from the freezer can become the star ingredient in this colorful and tasty dish.

Spaghetti *and* Shellfish

1 Bring a large pan of lightly salted water to a boil. Add the pasta, bring back to a boil, and cook for 8–10 minutes until tender, but still firm to the bite. Drain, then return to the pan, and stir in the oil. Keep warm.

2 Bring the bouillon and lemon juice to a boil. Add the cauliflower and carrots and cook for 3–4 minutes until barely tender. Remove with a slotted spoon and set aside. Add the snow peas and cook for 1–2 minutes until they begin to soften. Remove with a slotted spoon and add to the other vegetables. Reserve the bouillon for future use.

3 Melt half of the butter in a skillet over medium heat and cook the onion and zucchini for about 3 minutes. Add the garlic and shrimp and cook for a further 2–3 minutes until thoroughly heated through.

4 Stir in the reserved vegetables and heat through. Season to taste with salt and pepper, then stir in the remaining butter.

5 Transfer the spaghetti to a warmed serving dish. Pour on the sauce and sprinkle with parsley. Toss well, using 2 forks, until thoroughly coated. Sprinkle on the grated cheese and paprika, and garnish with unshelled shrimp, if using. Serve immediately.

SERVES 4

8 oz/225 g dried short-cut spaghetti
1 tbsp olive oil
1¼ cups chicken bouillon
1 tsp lemon juice
1 small cauliflower, cut into flowerets
2 carrots, thinly sliced
1½ cups snow peas
4 tbsp butter
1 onion, sliced
2 cups thinly sliced zucchini
1 garlic clove, chopped
12 oz/350 g frozen shelled shrimp, thawed
2 tbsp chopped fresh parsley
⅓ cup grated Parmesan cheese
½ tsp paprika
salt and pepper
4 unshelled shrimp, to garnish (optional)

NUTRITION
Calories 510; Sugars 38 g; Protein 33 g; Carbohydrate 44 g; Fat 24 g; Saturates 11 g

✪✪✪   moderate
🕐   20 mins
🕐   25 mins

The smoked salmon ideally complements the spaghetti to give a very luxurious dish.

Spaghetti *and* Salmon Sauce

SERVES 4

1 lb/450 g buckwheat spaghetti
2 tbsp olive oil
½ cup feta cheese, crumbled
fresh cilantro or parsley, to garnish

sauce

1¼ cups heavy cream
⅔ cup whiskey or brandy
4 oz/125 g smoked salmon
large pinch of cayenne pepper
2 tbsp chopped cilantro or parsley
salt and pepper

1 Cook the spaghetti in a large pan of salted boiling water, adding 1 tablespoon of the olive oil, for 8–10 minutes or until tender. Drain the pasta in a colander. Return the pasta to the pan, sprinkle over the remaining oil, cover and shake the pan. Set aside and keep warm until required.

2 In separate small pans, heat the cream and the whiskey to simmering point to make the sauce. Do not let them boil.

3 Combine the cream with the whiskey or brandy.

4 Cut the smoked salmon into thin strips and add to the cream mixture. Season with a little pepper and cayenne pepper to taste, and then stir in the cilantro or parsley.

5 Transfer the spaghetti to a warmed serving dish, pour on the sauce and toss thoroughly using 2 large forks. Scatter the crumbled cheese over the pasta and garnish with the cilantro. Serve at once.

NUTRITION
Calories *782*; Sugars *3 g*; Protein *20 g*;
Carbohydrate *48 g*; Fat *48 g*; Saturates *27 g*

very easy

10 mins

15 mins

COOK'S TIP

You can substitute linguine, fettuccine, or any other long pasta for the spaghetti, if preferred.

Serve this aromatic seafood dish with plenty of fresh, crusty bread to soak up the delicious sauce.

Pasta *and* Mussel Sauce

1 Pull off the "beards" from the mussels and rinse well in several changes of water. Discard any mussels that do not close when tapped. Put the mussels in a large pan with the white wine and half the onions. Cover the pan, shake and cook over a medium heat for 2–3 minutes until the mussels open.

2 Remove the pan from the heat, lift out the mussels with a draining spoon, reserving the liquor, and set aside until they are cool enough to handle. Discard any mussels that have not opened.

3 Melt the butter in a pan over medium heat and pan-fry the remaining onion for 3–4 minutes or until translucent. Stir in the garlic and cook for 1 minute. Gradually pour on the reserved cooking liquor, stirring to blend thoroughly. Stir in the parsley and cream. Season to taste and bring to simmering point. Taste and adjust the seasoning if necessary.

4 Cook the pasta in a large pan of salted boiling water, adding the oil, for 8–10 minutes or until tender. Drain the pasta in a colander, return to the pan, cover and keep warm.

5 Remove the mussels from their shells, reserving a few shells for garnish. Stir the mussels into the cream sauce. Tip the pasta into a warmed serving dish, pour on the sauce and, using 2 large spoons, toss it together well. Garnish with a few of the reserved mussel shells. Serve hot, with warm, crusty bread.

SERVES 6

4 ½ cups pasta shells (conchiglie)
1 tbsp olive oil

sauce

6 pints/3.5 liters mussels, scrubbed
1 cup dry white wine
2 large onions, chopped
½ cup unsalted butter
6 large garlic cloves, finely chopped
5 tbsp chopped fresh parsley
1 ¼ cups heavy cream
salt and pepper
crusty bread, to serve

NUTRITION
Calories *735*; Sugars *3 g*; Protein *37 g*;
Carbohydrate *41 g*; Fat *46 g*; Saturates *26 g*

 easy

25 mins

 25 mins

This Sicilian recipe of anchovies mixed with pinenuts and golden raisins in a tomato sauce is delicious with all types of pasta.

Pasta *and* Sicilian Sauce

SERVES 4

½ cup golden raisins
1 lb/450 g tomatoes, halved
¼ cup pinenuts
1 ¾ oz/50 g canned anchovies, drained and
    halved lengthways
2 tbsp concentrated tomato paste
1 ½ lb/675 g fresh or
    12 oz/350 g dried penne

1 Soak the golden raisins in a bowl of warm water for about 20 minutes. Drain the fruit thoroughly.

2 Meanwhile, cook the tomatoes under a preheated broiler for about 10 minutes. Let cool slightly, then once cool enough to handle, peel off the skin and dice the flesh.

3 Place the pinenuts on a cookie sheet and lightly toast under the broiler for 2–3 minutes or until golden brown.

4 Place the tomatoes, pinenuts and golden raisins in a small pan and gently heat through.

5 Add the anchovies and tomato paste, heating the sauce for a further 2–3 minutes or until hot.

6 Cook the pasta in a pan of salted boiling water for 8–10 minutes or until it is cooked through, but still has "bite." Drain thoroughly.

7 Transfer the pasta to a serving plate and serve with the hot Sicilian sauce.

NUTRITION
Calories *286*; Sugars *14 g*; Protein *11 g*;
Carbohydrate *46 g*; Fat *8 g*; Saturates *1 g*

⭐⭐   easy
🕐   25 mins
🕐   35 mins

 COOK'S TIP

Add 4 oz/115 g bacon, broiled for 5 minutes until crispy, then chopped, instead of the anchovies, if you prefer.

Fresh clams are available from most good fish stores. If you prefer, used canned clams, which are less messy to eat, but not so pretty to serve.

Pasta *with* Clams *and* White Wine

1 If you are using fresh clams, scrub them clean and discard any that are already open.

2 Heat the oil in a large skillet. Add the garlic and the clams to the pan and cook for 2 minutes, shaking the pan to ensure that all of the clams are coated in the oil.

3 Add the remaining seafood mixture to the pan and cook for an additional 2 minutes.

4 Pour the wine and bouillon over the mixed seafood and garlic and bring to a boil. Cover the pan, then reduce the heat and let simmer for 8–10 minutes or until the shells open. Discard any clams or mussels that do not open.

5 Meanwhile, cook the pasta in a pan of salted boiling water according to the pack instructions, or until it is cooked through, but still has "bite." Drain.

6 Stir the tarragon into the sauce and season to taste.

7 Transfer the pasta to a serving plate and pour over the sauce.

SERVES 4

1 lb 8 oz/675 g fresh clams or 10 oz/285 g canned clams, drained
2 tbsp olive oil
2 garlic cloves, finely chopped
1 lb/450 g mixed seafood, such as shrimps, squid, and mussels, thawed if frozen
$^2/_3$ cup white wine
$^2/_3$ cup fish bouillon
2 tbsp chopped fresh tarragon
salt and pepper
1 lb 8 oz/675 g fresh pasta or 12 oz/350 g dried pasta

NUTRITION
Calories *410*; Sugars *1 g*; Protein *39 g*;
Carbohydrate *39 g*; Fat *9 g*; Saturates *1 g*

  easy

 20 mins

🕐 25 mins

🍳 **COOK'S TIP**

Red clam sauce can be made by adding 8 tablespoons of crushed tomatoes to the sauce along with the bouillon in step 4. Follow the same cooking method.

This is a recipe to look forward to when parsley is at its most prolific, in the growing season.

Spaghetti, Tuna, *and* Parsley

SERVES 4

1 lb/450 g spaghetti
1 tbsp olive oil
2 tbsp butter

sauce

7 oz/200 g canned tuna, drained
2 oz/55 g canned anchovies, drained
1 cup olive oil
1 cup roughly chopped fresh, flatleaf parsley
²⁄₃ cup heavy cream
salt and pepper
fresh parsley, to garnish

1 Cook the spaghetti in a large saucepan of salted boiling water, with the olive oil, for 8–10 minutes or until tender. Drain the spaghetti in a colander and return to the pan. Add the butter, toss thoroughly to coat and keep warm until required.

2 Flake the tuna into smaller pieces using 2 forks. Put it in a blender or food processor with the anchovies, olive oil and parsley and process until the sauce is smooth. Pour in the heavy cream and process for a few seconds to blend. Taste the sauce and season with salt and pepper.

3 Warm 4 plates. Shake the pan of spaghetti over a medium heat for a few minutes or until it is thoroughly warmed through.

4 Pour the sauce over the spaghetti and toss quickly, using 2 forks. Serve immediately, garnished with parsley.

NUTRITION

Calories *970*; Sugars *2 g*; Protein *23 g*;
Carbohydrate *42 g*; Fat *80 g*; Saturates *18 g*

 very easy

10 mins

 15 mins

🍳 **COOK'S TIP**

You can replace the spaghetti with any other long pasta shape, if preferred.

The creamy, nutty flavor of squash complements the *al dente* texture of the pasta. This recipe has been adapted for the microwave oven.

Penne *and* Butternut Squash

1 Combine the olive oil, garlic, and bread crumbs and spread out on a large plate. Cook in the microwave on high power for 4–5 minutes, stirring every minute, until crisp and beginning to brown. Remove from the microwave and set aside.

2 Place the squash in a large bowl with half of the water. Cover and cook on high power for 8–9 minutes, stirring occasionally. Stand for 2 minutes.

3 Place the pasta in a large bowl, add a little salt, and pour over boiling water to cover by 1 inch/2.5 cm. Cover and cook on high power for 5 minutes, stirring once, until the pasta is just tender, but still firm to the bite. Stand, covered, for 1 minute before draining.

4 Place the butter and onion in a large bowl. Cover and cook on high power for 3 minutes.

5 Coarsely mash the squash, using a fork. Add to the onion with the pasta, ham, cream, cheese, parsley, and remaining water. Season generously and mix well. Cover and cook on high power for 4 minutes until thoroughly heated through.

6 Serve the pasta sprinkled with the crisp garlic crumbs.

SERVES 4

2 tbsp olive oil
1 garlic clove, crushed
1 cup fresh white bread crumbs
1 lb/450 g butternut squash, peeled, seeded, and diced
8 tbsp water
1 lb/450 g fresh penne, or other pasta shapes
1 tbsp butter
1 onion, sliced
4 oz/100 g ham, cut into strips
scant 1 cup light cream
½ cup grated colby cheese
2 tbsp chopped fresh parsley
salt and pepper

NUTRITION
Calories *499*; Sugars *4 g*; Protein *20 g*; Carbohydrate *49 g*; Fat *26 g*; Saturates *13 g*

⊗⊗ easy

◷ 15 mins

◷ 30 mins

Any variety of long pasta could be used for this very tasty dish from Sicily.

Sicilian Spaghetti Cake

SERVES 4

2 eggplants, about 1 lb 8 oz/675 g in total
²/₃ cup olive oil
1½ cups finely ground beef
1 onion, chopped
2 garlic cloves, crushed
2 tbsp tomato paste
2 cups canned chopped tomatoes
1 tsp Worcestershire sauce
1 tsp chopped fresh oregano or marjoram or
    ½ tsp dried oregano or marjoram
⅓ cup pitted black olives, sliced
1 green, red or yellow bell pepper, halved,
    seeded and chopped
6 oz/175 g spaghetti
1 cup Parmesan cheese, grated

NUTRITION
Calories *876*; Sugars *10 g*; Protein *37 g*;
Carbohydrate *39 g*; Fat *65 g*; Saturates *18 g*

    moderate

30 mins

1 hr 10 mins

1 Brush an 8-inch/20-cm loose-based round cake pan with olive oil, place a disc of baking parchment in the base and brush with oil. Trim the eggplants and cut into slanting slices, ¼ inch/5 mm thick. Heat some of the oil in a skillet. Pan-fry a few slices of eggplant at a time until lightly browned, turning once, and adding more oil as necessary. Drain on paper towels.

2 Put the ground beef, onion, and garlic into a pan and cook, stirring frequently, until browned all over. Add the tomato paste, tomatoes, Worcestershire sauce, herbs, and seasoning. Simmer for 10 minutes, stirring occasionally, then add the olives and bell pepper and cook for 10 minutes.

3 Bring a large pan of salted water to a boil. Cook the spaghetti for 8–10 minutes, until just tender. Drain the spaghetti thoroughly. Turn the spaghetti into a bowl and mix in the meat mixture and Parmesan cheese, tossing together with 2 forks.

4 Lay overlapping slices of eggplant over the base of the cake pan and up the sides. Add the meat mixture, pressing it down, and cover with the remaining eggplant slices.

5 Stand the cake pan in a baking pan and cook in a preheated oven, 400°F/200°C, for 40 minutes. Let stand for 5 minutes then loosen around the edges and invert onto a warmed serving dish, releasing the pan clip. Remove the baking parchment. Serve immediately.

The sauce in this delicious baked pasta dish can also be used as an alternative sauce for Spaghetti Bolognese.

Lasagna Verde

1 Make the Ragu Sauce, but cook for 10–12 minutes longer than the time given, in an uncovered pan, to allow the excess liquid to evaporate. It needs to be reduced to the consistency of a thick paste.

2 Have ready a large pan of salted boiling water and add the olive oil. Drop the pasta sheets into the boiling water, a few at a time, and return the water to a boil before adding further pasta sheets. If you are using fresh lasagna, cook the sheets for a total of 8 minutes. If you are using dried or partly pre-cooked pasta, cook it according to the package instructions.

3 Remove the pasta sheets from the pan with a draining spoon. Spread them out in a single layer on clean, damp dish towels to prevent them from sticking.

4 Grease a rectangular casserole, 10–11 inches/25–28 cm long. To assemble the dish, spoon a little of the meat sauce into the prepared dish, cover with a layer of lasagna, then spoon over a little Béchamel Sauce, and sprinkle with some of the cheese. Continue making layers in this way, covering the final layer of lasagna sheets with the remaining Béchamel Sauce.

5 Sprinkle on the remaining cheese and bake in a preheated oven, 375°F/ 190°C, for 40 minutes or until the sauce is golden brown and bubbling. Serve with salad greens, a tomato salad, or a bowl of black olives.

SERVES 6

1 quantity Ragu Sauce (see page 9)
1 tbsp olive oil
8 oz/225 g lasagna verde
butter, for greasing
Béchamel Sauce (see page 14)
2/3 cup freshly grated Parmesan cheese
salt
salad greens, tomato salad, or black olives, to serve

NUTRITION
Calories 619; Sugars 7 g; Protein 29 g; Carbohydrate 21 g; Fat 45 g; Saturates 19 g

 challenging
1 hr 30 mins
1 hr

A recipe that has both Italian and Greek origins, this dish may be served hot or cold, cut into thick, satisfying squares.

Pasticcio

SERVES 6

3½ cups fusilli, or other short pasta shapes
1 tbsp olive oil
4 tbsp heavy cream
salt
fresh rosemary sprigs, to garnish

meat sauce

2 tbsp olive oil, plus extra for brushing
1 onion, thinly sliced
1 red bell pepper, seeded and chopped
2 garlic cloves, chopped
1 lb 8 oz/675 g lean ground beef
2 cups canned chopped tomatoes
½ cup dry white wine
2 tbsp chopped fresh parsley
1¾ oz/50 g canned anchovies, drained and chopped
salt and pepper

topping

1/4 cups unsweetened yogurt
3 eggs
pinch of freshly grated nutmeg
⅔ cup freshly grated Parmesan cheese

NUTRITION

Calories *590*; Sugars *8 g*; Protein *34 g*;
Carbohydrate *23 g*; Fat *39 g*; Saturates *16 g*

  easy

35 mins

1 hr 15 mins

1 To make the sauce, heat the oil in a large skillet and pan-fry the onion and bell pepper for 3 minutes. Stir in the garlic and cook for 1 minute. Add the beef and cook, stirring frequently, until browned.

2 Add the tomatoes and wine, stir well, and bring to a boil. Simmer, uncovered, for 20 minutes or until the sauce is fairly thick. Stir in the parsley and anchovies and season to taste.

3 Bring a large pan of lightly salted water to a boil. Add the oil and pasta, bring back to a boil, and cook for 8–10 minutes until tender, but still firm to the bite. Drain, then transfer to a bowl. Stir in the cream and set aside.

4 To make the topping, beat the yogurt with the eggs and nutmeg until well combined and season with salt and pepper to taste.

5 Brush a shallow casserole with oil. Spoon in half of the pasta and cover with half of the meat sauce. Repeat these layers, then spread the topping evenly over the final layer. Sprinkle the grated cheese evenly on top.

6 Bake in a preheated oven, 375°F/190°C, for 25 minutes or until the topping is golden brown and bubbling. Garnish with rosemary sprigs and serve.

COOK'S TIP

Serve this delicious dish with a selection of raw vegetable crudités to freshen the palate.

This variation of the traditional beef dish has layers of pasta, and chicken or turkey, baked in red wine, tomatoes, and a delicious cheese sauce.

Chicken *and* Tomato Lasagna

1 Cook the lasagna according to the package instructions. Lightly grease a deep ovenproof dish.

2 Heat the oil in a pan. Add the onion and garlic and cook for 3–4 minutes. Add the mushrooms and chicken and stir-fry for 4 minutes or until the meat is browned all over.

3 Add the wine, bring to a boil, then simmer for 5 minutes. Stir in the crushed tomatoes and sugar, and cook for 3–5 minutes until the meat is tender and cooked through. The sauce should be thick, but quite runny.

4 To make the cheese sauce, melt the butter in a pan, stir in the flour, and cook for 2 minutes. Remove the pan from the heat and gradually add the milk, mixing to form a smooth sauce. Return the pan to the heat and bring to a boil, stirring until thickened. Let cool slightly, then beat in the egg and half of the cheese. Season to taste.

5 Place 3 sheets of lasagna in the bottom of the dish and spread with half of the chicken mixture. Repeat the layers. Top with the last 3 sheets of lasagna, pour over the cheese sauce, and sprinkle with the Parmesan cheese. Bake in a preheated oven, at 375°F/190°C, for 30 minutes until golden and the pasta is cooked.

SERVES 4

12 oz/350 g fresh lasagna or 5½ oz/150 g dried lasagna (about 9 sheets)
butter, for greasing
1 tbsp olive oil
1 red onion, finely chopped
1 garlic clove, crushed
2 cups sliced mushrooms
12 oz/350 g chicken or turkey breast, cut into chunks
⅔ cup red wine, diluted with scant ⅓ cup water
1 cup crushed tomatoes
1 tsp sugar

cheese sauce
5 tbsp butter
6 tbsp all-purpose flour
2½ cups milk
1 egg, beaten
1 cup freshly grated Parmesan cheese
salt and pepper

NUTRITION
Calories *550*; Sugars *11 g*; Protein *35 g*; Carbohydrate *34 g*; Fat *29 g*; Saturates *12 g*

★★★ moderate
🕑 20 mins
🕐 1 hr 15 mins

There is an appetizing contrast of textures and flavors in this satisfying family dish, which has now become known the world over.

Tagliatelle *with* Meatballs

SERVES 4

1 lb/450 g ground lean beef
1 cup soft white bread crumbs
1 garlic clove, crushed
2 tbsp chopped fresh parsley
1 tsp dried oregano
pinch of freshly grated nutmeg
1/4 tsp ground coriander
2/3 cup freshly grated Parmesan cheese
2–3 tbsp milk
all-purpose flour, for dusting
3 tbsp olive oil
14 oz/400 g dried tagliatelle
2 tbsp butter, diced
salt and pepper

sauce
3 tbsp olive oil
2 large onions, sliced
2 celery stalks, thinly sliced
2 garlic cloves, chopped
2 cups canned chopped tomatoes
4 1/2 oz/125 g sun-dried tomatoes, chopped
2 tbsp tomato paste
1 tbsp molasses sugar
2/3 cup white wine or water

NUTRITION
Calories *910*; Sugars *13 g*; Protein *40 g*;
Carbohydrate *65 g*; Fat *54 g*; Saturates *19 g*

moderate

45 mins

1 hr 5 mins

1 To make the sauce, heat the oil in a skillet. Add the onions and celery and cook until translucent. Add the garlic and cook for 1 minute. Stir in the tomatoes, tomato paste, sugar, and wine, and season to taste with salt and pepper. Bring to a boil and simmer for 10 minutes.

2 Meanwhile, break up the meat in a bowl with a wooden spoon, until it becomes a sticky paste. Stir in the bread crumbs, garlic, herbs, and spices. Stir in the cheese and enough milk to make a firm paste. Flour your hands, take large spoonfuls of the mixture, and shape it into 12 balls. Heat the oil in a skillet and fry the meatballs for 5–6 minutes until browned.

3 Pour the tomato sauce over the meatballs. Lower the heat, cover the pan, and simmer for 30 minutes, turning once or twice. Add a little extra water if the sauce is beginning to become dry.

4 Bring a large pan of lightly salted water to a boil. Add the pasta, bring back to a boil, and cook for 8–10 minutes, until tender, but still firm to the bite. Drain the pasta, then turn into a warmed serving dish, dot with the butter, and toss with two forks. Spoon the meatballs and sauce over the pasta and serve immediately.

COOK'S TIP

Check the sauce and meatballs regularly to make sure they aren't sticking to the pan and add a little extra water to the sauce, if necessary.

These tasty little squares of pasta stuffed with mushrooms and cheese are surprisingly filling. Serve about three pieces for an appetizer and up to nine for a main course.

Cheesy Pasta Squares

1 Using a serrated pasta cutter, cut 2-inch/5-cm squares from the sheets of fresh pasta. To make 36 tortelloni, you will need 72 squares. Once the pasta is cut, cover the squares with plastic wrap to stop them drying out.

2 Heat 3 tablespoons of the butter in a skillet. Add the shallots, 1 minced garlic clove, the mushrooms, and celery, and cook for 4–5 minutes.

3 Remove the pan from the heat, then stir in the cheese and season.

4 Spoon half a teaspoon of the mixture on to the middle of 36 pasta squares. Brush the edges of the squares with water and top with the remaining 36 squares. Press the edges together to seal. Let rest for 5 minutes.

5 Bring a large pan of salted water to a boil, then add the oil and cook the tortelloni, in batches, for 2–3 minutes. The tortelloni will rise to the surface when cooked and the pasta should be tender with a slight bite. Remove from the pan with a draining spoon and drain thoroughly.

6 Meanwhile, melt the remaining butter in a pan. Add the remaining garlic and plenty of pepper and cook for 1–2 minutes.

7 Transfer the tortelloni to serving plates and pour over the garlic butter. Garnish with extra grated romano cheese and serve immediately.

SERVES 4

10 oz/280 g Basic Pasta Dough (see page 9), rolled into thin sheets
5 tbsp butter
½ cup finely chopped shallots
3 garlic cloves, minced
½ cup finely chopped mushrooms
½ celery stalk, finely chopped
¼ cup finely grated romano cheese, plus extra to garnish
1 tbsp oil
salt and pepper

NUTRITION
Calories *360*; Sugars *1 g*; Protein *9 g*; Carbohydrate *36 g*; Fat *21 g*; Saturates *12 g*

 challenging
1 hr 15 mins
25 mins

Pizzas *and* Breads

Few things can beat the irresistible aroma and taste of a freshly-made pizza cooked in a wood-fired oven. The recipes for the homemade dough base and freshly made tomato sauce in this chapter will give you the closest thing possible to an authentic Italian pizza. You can add any type of topping, from salamis and cooked meats, to vegetables and fragrant herbs—the choice is yours!

Traditionally, pizza bases are made from bread dough; this recipe will give you a base similar to an Italian pizza.

Bread Dough Base

SERVES 4

15 g/½ oz fresh yeast or 1 tsp dried or rapid rise dry yeast
6 tbsp lukewarm water
½ tsp sugar
1 tbsp olive oil
1½ cups all-purpose flour, plus extra for dusting
1 tsp salt

1 Combine the fresh yeast with the water and sugar in a bowl. If using dry yeast, sprinkle it over the surface of the water and whisk in until dissolved.

2 Set aside in a warm place for 10–15 minutes until frothy on the surface. Stir in the olive oil.

3 Strain the flour and salt into a large bowl. If using easy-blend yeast, stir it in. Make a well in the center and pour in the yeast liquid, or water and oil (without the sugar for dry yeast).

4 Using either floured hands or a wooden spoon, mix together to form a dough. Turn out onto a floured counter and knead for about 5 minutes, until smooth and elastic.

5 Place the dough in a large greased plastic bag and set aside in a warm place for about 1 hour or until doubled in size. Heated closets are often the best places for this process, as the temperature remains constant.

6 Turn out onto a lightly floured work surface and punch down the dough. This releases any air bubbles which would make the pizza uneven. Knead four or five times. The dough is now ready to use.

NUTRITION
Calories *182*; Sugars *2 g*; Protein *5 g*; Carbohydrate *36 g*; Fat *3 g*; Saturates *0.5 g*

moderate

1 hr 30 mins

0 mins

This is a quicker alternative to the bread dough base. If you do not have time to wait for bread dough to rise, a biscuit base is ideal.

Biscuit Base

1 Sift the flour and salt into a large mixing bowl.

2 Rub in the butter with your fingertips until it resembles fine bread crumbs.

3 Make a well in the center of the flour and butter mixture and pour in nearly all of the milk at once. Mix in quickly with a knife. Add the remaining milk only if necessary to mix to a soft dough.

4 Turn the dough out on to a floured counter and knead by turning and pressing with the heel of your hand three or four times.

5 Either roll out or press the dough into a 10-inch/25-cm circle on a lightly greased cookie sheet or pizza pan. Push up the edge slightly all round to form a ridge and use immediately.

SERVES 4

scant 1½ cups self-rising flour
½ tsp salt
2 tbsp butter
½ cup milk

🙂 **COOK'S TIP**

Keep utensils and ingredients as cool as possible and use a light touch for the best results when making biscuit base.

NUTRITION
Calories *215*; Sugars *3 g*; Protein *5 g*;
Carbohydrate *35 g*; Fat *7 g*; Saturates *4 g*

⭐⭐ easy
🕐 20 mins
🕐 0 mins

This is an unusual pizza base made from mashed potatoes and flour and is a great way to use up any leftover boiled potatoes.

Potato Base

SERVES 4

1 cup mashed potatoes
¼ cup butter or margarine
1 cup self-rising flour
½ tsp salt

1   If the mashed potatoes are hot, stir in the butter until it has melted and is distributed evenly throughout the potatoes. Leave to cool.

2   Sift the flour and salt together and stir into the mashed potato to form a soft dough.

3   If the mashed potatoes are cold, do not add butter at this stage. Sift the flour and salt into a bowl.

4   Rub in the butter with your fingertips until the mixture resembles fine breadcrumbs, then stir the flour and butter mixture into the mashed potatoes to form a soft dough.

5   Either roll out or press the dough into a 10-inch/25-cm circle on a lightly greased cookie sheet or pizza pan, pushing up the edge slightly all round to form a ridge before adding the topping of your choice. This potato base is rather tricky to lift before it is cooked, so you will find it much easier to handle if you roll it out directly onto the cookie sheet.

6   If the base is not required for cooking immediately, cover it with plastic wrap and chill it for up to 2 hours.

NUTRITION
Calories *170*; Sugars *1 g*; Protein *4 g*;
Carbohydrate *34 g*; Fat *3 g*; Saturates *1 g*

moderate

2 hrs 15 mins

0 mins

This is a basic topping sauce for pizzas. Using canned chopped tomatoes for this dish saves time.

Tomato Sauce

1 Pan-fry the onion and garlic gently in the oil for 5 minutes or until softened but not browned.

2 Add the tomatoes, tomato paste, sugar, oregano, bay leaf, and salt and pepper to taste. Stir well.

3 Bring the sauce to a boil, cover and leave to simmer gently for 20 minutes, stirring occasionally, until you have a thickish sauce.

4 Remove the bay leaf and season to taste with salt and pepper. Leave to cool completely before using. This sauce keeps well in a screw-top jar in the refrigerator for up to 1 week.

SERVES 4

1 small onion, chopped
1 garlic clove, crushed
1 tbsp olive oil
1 cup canned chopped tomatoes
2 tsp tomato paste
½ tsp sugar
½ tsp dried oregano
1 bay leaf
salt and pepper

NUTRITION
Calories 41; Sugars 3 g; Protein 1 g; Carbohydrate 3 g; Fat 3 g; Saturates 0.4 g

 very easy

5 mins

 25 mins

👨‍🍳 COOK'S TIP

You can use fresh tomatoes for this dish, if you prefer, but choose ripe plum tomatoes and increase the cooking time so the sauce thickens nicely and the tomatoes soften enough.

This sauce is made with fresh tomatoes. Use the plum variety whenever available and always choose the reddest ones for the best flavor.

Special Tomato Sauce

SERVES 4

1 small onion, chopped
1 small red bell pepper, halved, seeded, and chopped
1 garlic clove, crushed
2 tbsp olive oil
2–3 tomatoes
1 tbsp tomato paste
1 tsp soft brown sugar
2 tsp chopped fresh basil
½ tsp dried oregano
1 bay leaf
salt and pepper

1 Pan-fry the onion, bell pepper, and garlic gently in the oil for 5 minutes until softened but not browned.

2 Cut a cross in the base of each tomato and place them in a bowl. Pour on boiling water and leave for about 45 seconds. Drain, and then plunge in cold water. The skins will slide off easily.

3 Chop the tomatoes, discarding any hard cores.

4 Add the tomatoes to the onion mixture with the tomato paste, sugar, herbs, and seasoning. Stir well. Bring to a boil, cover and leave to simmer gently for about 30 minutes, stirring occasionally, or until you have a thickish sauce.

5 Remove the bay leaf and adjust the seasoning to taste. Let cool completely before using.

6 The sauce will keep in a screw-top jar in the refrigerator for up to 1 week.

NUTRITION
Calories *81*; Sugars *6 g*; Protein *1 g*; Carbohydrate *6 g*; Fat *6 g*; Saturates *1 g*

easy
10 mins
35 mins

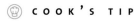 **COOK'S TIP**

As an alternative method of peeling tomatoes, hold the tomato over a naked flame using a fork until the skin blisters. It should then peel off easily.

Pizza means "pie" in Italian. The fresh bread dough is not difficult to make, but it does take a little time.

Pizza Margarita

1 Place the yeast and sugar in a pitcher and mix with 4 tablespoons of the water. Let the yeast mixture stand in a warm place for 15 minutes, or until it becomes frothy.

2 Mix the flour in a bowl, with the salt and make a well in the center. Add the oil, the yeast mixture, and the remaining water. Using a wooden spoon, mix together to form a dough.

3 Turn the dough out onto a floured counter and knead for 4–5 minutes, or until smooth.

4 Return the dough to the bowl, then cover with an oiled sheet of plastic wrap and let rise for 30 minutes, or until doubled in size.

5 Knead the dough for 2 minutes. Stretch the dough with your hands, then place it on an oiled cookie sheet, pushing out the edges until even and to the shape required. The dough should be no more than $\frac{1}{4}$ inch thick because it will rise during cooking.

6 To make the topping, place the tomatoes, garlic, dried basil, olive oil, and salt and pepper to taste in a large skillet and let simmer for 20 minutes, or until the sauce has thickened. Stir in the tomato paste and let cool slightly.

7 Spread the topping evenly over the pizza base. Top with the mozzarella and Parmesan cheeses and bake in a preheated oven, 400°F/200°C, for 20–25 minutes. Serve hot.

SERVES **4**

basic pizza dough
$\frac{1}{4}$ oz rapid rise dry yeast
1 tsp sugar
1 cup hand-hot water
12 oz/350 g strong flour
1 tsp salt
1 tbsp olive oil

topping
2 cups canned chopped tomatoes
2 garlic cloves, minced
2 tsp dried basil
1 tbsp olive oil
2 tbsp tomato paste
1 cup chopped mozzarella cheese
2 tbsp freshly grated Parmesan cheese
salt and pepper

NUTRITION
Calories *456*; Sugars *7 g*; Protein *16 g*;
Carbohydrate *74 g*; Fat *13 g*; Saturates *5 g*

moderate

1 hr

45 mins

Wonderfully colorful vegetables are roasted in olive oil with thyme and garlic. The goat cheese adds a nutty, piquant flavor.

Vegetable *and* Goat Cheese Pizza

SERVES 4

2 baby zucchini, halved lengthwise
2 baby eggplants, halved, seeded, and quartered lengthwise
½ red bell pepper, halved, seeded, and cut into 4 strips
½ yellow bell pepper, halved, seeded and cut into 4 strips
1 small red onion, cut into wedges
2 garlic cloves, unpeeled
4 tbsp olive oil
1 tbsp red wine vinegar
1 tbsp chopped fresh thyme
1 quantity Bread Dough Base (see page 156)
1 quantity Special Tomato Sauce (see page 160)
⅔ cup crumbled goat cheese
salt and pepper
fresh basil leaves, to garnish

NUTRITION
Calories *387*; Sugars *9 g*; Protein *10 g*;
Carbohydrate *42 g*; Fat *21 g*; Saturates *5 g*

 moderate

2 hrs 30 mins

40 mins

1 Place all of the prepared vegetables in a large roasting pan. Mix together the olive oil, vinegar, thyme, and plenty of seasoning and pour over, coating well.

2 Roast the vegetables in a preheated oven, at 400°F/200°C, for 15–20 minutes or until the skins have started to blacken in places, turning half-way through. Leave to rest for 5 minutes after roasting.

3 Carefully peel off the skins from the roast bell peppers and the garlic cloves. Slice the garlic.

4 Roll out or press the dough, using a rolling pin or your hands, into a 10 inch/25 cm circle on a lightly floured counter. Place on a large greased cookie sheet or pizza pan and raise the edge a little. Cover and leave for 10 minutes to rise slightly in a warm place. Spread with the Special Tomato Sauce almost to the edge.

5 Arrange the roasted vegetables on top and dot with the cheese. Drizzle the oil and juices from the roasting pan over the pizza and season.

6 Bake in a preheated oven, at 400°F/200°C , for 18–20 minutes, or until the edge is crisp and golden. Serve immediately, garnished with basil leaves.

Juicy mushrooms and stringy mozzarella top this tomato-based pizza. Use wild mushrooms or a combination of wild and cultivated mushrooms.

Mushroom Pizza

1 Knead the dough for 2 minutes. Using a rolling pin, roll out the dough to form an oval or a circular shape, then place it on an oiled baking pan, pushing out the edges until even. The dough should be no more than ¼ inch/5 mm thick because it will rise during cooking.

2 To make the topping, place the tomatoes, garlic, dried basil, olive oil, and salt and pepper in a large pan and simmer for 20 minutes, or until the sauce has thickened. Stir in the tomato paste and leave to cool slightly.

3 Spread the sauce evenly over the base of the pizza, top with the sliced mushrooms and scatter over the grated mozzarella.

4 Bake in a preheated oven, 400°F/200°C, for 25 minutes. Just before serving, garnish with fresh basil leaves.

SERVES 4

1 quantity Basic Pizza Dough (see page 161)

topping
2 cups canned chopped tomatoes
2 garlic cloves, crushed
1 tsp dried basil
1 tbsp olive oil
2 tbsp tomato paste
7 oz/200 g mushrooms, sliced
1 ½ cups grated mozzarella cheese
salt and pepper
basil leaves, to garnish

NUTRITION
Calories *302*; Sugars *7 g*; Protein *10 g*;
Carbohydrate *41 g*; Fat *12 g*; Saturates *4 g*

moderate
1 hr 15 mins
45 mins

COOK'S TIP

You can just as easily make smaller, individual pizzas—just reduce the cooking time slightly.

The vibrant colors of the bell peppers and red onion make this a delightful pizza. Served cut into fingers, it is ideal for a party or buffet.

Californian Pepper Pizza

SERVES 8

1 quantity Bread Dough Base (see page 156)
2 tbsp olive oil, plus extra for drizzling
½ red bell pepper, halved, seeded, and thinly sliced
½ green bell pepper, halved, seeded, and thinly sliced
½ yellow bell pepper, halved, seeded, and thinly sliced
1 small red onion, thinly sliced
1 garlic clove, crushed
Special Tomato Sauce (see page 160)
3 tbsp raisins
4 tbsp pinenuts
1 tbsp chopped fresh thyme
salt and pepper

1 Roll out or press the dough, using a rolling pin or your hands, on a lightly floured counter to fit a 12 x 7-inch/ 30 x 18-cm greased jelly roll pan. Place the dough in the pan and push up the edges slightly.

2 Cover with plastic wrap and set the dough aside in a warm place for about 10 minutes to rise slightly.

3 Heat the oil in a large skillet. Add the bell peppers, onion, and garlic and cook gently for 5 minutes, until they have softened. Set aside to cool.

4 Spread the tomato sauce over the base of the pizza almost to the edge.

5 Sprinkle over the raisins and top with the cooled bell pepper mixture. Add the pinenuts and thyme. Drizzle with a little olive oil and season to taste with salt and pepper.

6 Bake in a preheated oven, 400°F/ 200°C, for 18–20 minutes, or until the edges are crisp and golden. Cut into fingers and serve immediately.

NUTRITION
Calories 380; Sugars 19 g; Protein 7 g;
Carbohydrate 53 g; Fat 17 g; Saturates 2 g

moderate

2 hrs 30 mins

25 mins

As the name implies, this colorful pizza should be topped with fresh vegetables from the garden, especially in the summer months.

Giardiniera Pizza

1 Remove any tough stalks from the spinach and wash the leaves in cold water. Pat dry with paper towels.

2 Roll out or press the pizza base, using a rolling pin or your hands, into a 10-inch/25-cm circle on a lightly floured counter. Place the round on a large greased cookie sheet or pizza pan and push up the edge a little. Spread with the Special Tomato Sauce.

3 Arrange the spinach leaves on the sauce, followed by the tomato slices. Top with the remaining vegetables and the fresh mixed herbs.

4 Combine the cheeses and sprinkle over the pizza. Place the artichoke heart in the center. Drizzle the pizza with a little olive oil and season to taste.

5 Bake in a preheated oven, 400°F/200°C, for 18–20 minutes or until the edges are crisp and golden brown. Serve immediately.

SERVES 4

6 spinach leaves
1 quantity Bread Dough Base (see page 156) or 1 x 10-inch/25-cm pizza base
1 quantity Basic Tomato Sauce (see page 159)
1 tomato, sliced
1 celery stalk, thinly sliced
½ green bell pepper, halved, seeded, and thinly sliced
1 baby zucchini, sliced
1 oz/25 g asparagus tips
2½ tbsp corn, thawed if frozen
4 tbsp peas, thawed if frozen
4 scallions, trimmed and chopped
1 tbsp chopped fresh mixed herbs
½ cup grated mozzarella cheese
2 tbsp freshly grated Parmesan cheese
1 artichoke heart
olive oil, for drizzling
salt and pepper

NUTRITION
Calories 362; Sugars 10 g; Protein 13 g; Carbohydrate 48 g; Fat 15 g; Saturates 5 g

 moderate

 2 hrs 30 mins

20 mins

🍳 **COOK'S TIP**

Use any mixture of fresh herbs for this pizza. Good combinations are basil, parsley, and mint, or oregano, parsley, and thyme.

This is a traditional dish from the Calabrian Mountains in southern Italy, where it is made with naturally sun-dried tomatoes and ricotta cheese.

Sun-dried Tomato *and* Ricotta Pizza

SERVES 4

1 quantity Basic Pizza Dough (see page 161)

topping
4 tbsp sun-dried tomato paste
⅔ cup ricotta cheese
10 sun-dried tomatoes, cut into strips
1 tbsp fresh thyme
salt and pepper

1 Knead the dough for 2 minutes.

2 Using a rolling pin, roll out the dough to form a circle, then place it on an oiled cookie sheet, pushing out the edges until even. The dough should be no more than ¼ inch/5 mm thick because it will rise during cooking.

3 Spread the sun-dried tomato paste over the dough, then add spoonfuls of the ricotta cheese all over.

4 Arrange the sun dried tomatoes on top of the pizza.

5 Sprinkle the thyme and salt and pepper to taste over the top of the pizza. Bake in a preheated oven, 400°F/200°C, for 30 minutes or until the crust is golden. Serve hot.

NUTRITION
Calories *274*; Sugars *4 g*; Protein *8 g*;
Carbohydrate *38 g*; Fat *11 g*; Saturates *4 g*

moderate

1hr 15 mins

30 mins

 COOK'S TIP

As an alternative to the ricotta cheese, use any soft cream cheese or creamy goats' cheese, which goes beatifully with sun-dried tomatoes.

A pizza adaptation of Eggs Florentine—sliced hard-cooked eggs on freshly cooked spinach, with a crunchy almond topping.

Florentine Pizza

1 Roll out or press the dough, using a rolling pin or your hands, into a 10-inch/25-cm circle on a lightly floured counter. Brush with the olive oil and sprinkle with the Parmesan cheese. Place on a large greased cookie sheet or pizza pan and push up the edge slightly. Spread the Special Tomato Sauce almost to the edge.

2 Remove the stalks from the spinach and wash the leaves thoroughly in plenty of water. Drain and pat off the excess water with paper towels.

3 Heat the remaining oil and cook the onion for 5 minutes until softened. Add the spinach and cook until just wilted. Drain off any excess liquid. Arrange on the pizza and sprinkle over the nutmeg.

4 Shell and slice the eggs. Arrange the slices of egg on top of the spinach.

5 Combine the bread crumbs, cheese, and almonds and sprinkle over. Drizzle with a little olive oil and season to taste.

6 Bake in a preheated oven, 400°F/200°C, for 18–20 minutes or until the edge is crisp and golden. Serve the pizza immediately.

SERVES 4

1 quantity Bread Dough Base (see page 156)
   or 1 x 10-inch/25-cm pizza base
3 tbsp olive oil, plus extra for drizzling
2 tbsp freshly grated Parmesan cheese
Special Tomato Sauce (see page 160)
6 oz/175 g spinach
1 small red onion, thinly sliced
¼ tsp freshly grated nutmeg
2 hard-cooked eggs
¼ cup fresh white bread crumbs
½ cup grated Jarlsberg, colby, or Swiss
   cheese, grated
2 tbsp sliced almonds
salt and pepper

NUTRITION
Calories *462*; Sugars *6 g*; Protein *18 g*;
Carbohydrate *41 g*; Fat *26 g*; Saturates *8 g*

⭐⭐⭐   moderate
🕐   2 hrs 30 mins
🕐   20 mins

This is a traditional pizza on which the toppings are divided into four sections, each of which is supposed to depict a season of the year.

Four Seasons Pizza

SERVES 4

1 quantity Bread Dough Base (see page 156)
Special Tomato Sauce (see page 160)
1 oz/25 g chorizo sausage, sliced thinly
½ cup button mushrooms, sliced thinly
1½ oz/45 g artichoke hearts, sliced thinly
¼ cup thinly sliced mozzarella
3 anchovies, halved lengthwise
2 tsp capers
4 pitted black olives, sliced
4 fresh basil leaves, shredded
olive oil, for drizzling
salt and pepper

1 Roll out or press the dough, using a rolling pin or your hands, into a 10-inch/25-cm circle on a lightly floured counter. Place on a large greased cookie sheet or pizza pan and push up the edge a little.

2 Cover and leave to rise slightly for 10 minutes in a warm place. Spread the Special Tomato Sauce over the pizza base, almost to the edge.

3 Put the sliced chorizo onto one fourth of the pizza, the sliced mushrooms on another, the artichoke hearts on a third, and the mozzarella and anchovies on the fourth.

4 Dot with the capers, olives and basil leaves. Drizzle with a little olive oil and season. Do not put any salt on the anchovy section as the fish are very salty.

5 Bake in a preheated oven, at 400°F/200°C, for 18–20 minutes, or until the crust is golden and crisp. Serve immediately.

NUTRITION
Calories *313*; Sugars *8 g*; Protein *8 g*;
Carbohydrate *44 g*; Fat *13 g*; Saturates *3 g*

moderate

2 hrs 45 mins

20 mins

An unusual fragrant, spiced pizza topped with ground lamb and eggplant on a bread base.

Eggplant *and* Lamb Pizza

1 Place the diced eggplant in a colander, sprinkle with the salt and let the bitter juices drain for about 20 minutes. Rinse thoroughly, then pat dry with paper towels.

2 Roll out or press the dough, using a rolling pin or your hands, into a 10-inch/25-cm circle on a lightly floured work surface. Place on a large greased cookie sheet or pizza pan and push up the edge to form a rim.

3 Cover and leave to rise slightly for 10 minutes in a warm place.

4 Pan-fry the onion, garlic, and cumin seeds gently in the oil for 3 minutes. Increase the heat slightly and add the lamb, eggplant, and pimiento. Cook for 5 minutes, stirring occasionally. Add the cilantro and season with salt and pepper to taste.

5 Spread the Special Tomato Sauce over the dough base, almost to the edge. Top with the lamb mixture.

6 Arrange the mozzarella slices on top. Drizzle over a little olive oil and season with salt and pepper.

7 Bake in a preheated oven, at 400°F/200°C, for 18–20 minutes, or until the crust is crisp and golden. Serve immediately.

SERVES 4

1 small eggplant, diced
1 quantity Bread Dough Base (see page 156)
1 small onion, sliced thinly
1 garlic clove, crushed
1 tsp cumin seeds
1 tbsp olive oil
6 oz/175 g ground lamb
1 oz/25 g canned pimiento, sliced thinly
2 tbsp chopped fresh cilantro
Special Tomato Sauce (see page 160)
¾ cup thinly sliced mozzarella
olive oil, for drizzling
salt and pepper

NUTRITION
Calories *430*; Sugars *10 g*; Protein *18 g*;
Carbohydrate *44 g*; Fat *22 g*; Saturates *7 g*

⭐⭐⭐   moderate

🕐   2 hrs 30 mins

🕐   30 mins

This more traditional kind
of pizza is topped with
pepperoni, smoked bacon
and bell peppers,
and covered in a
smoked cheese.

Smoky Bacon *and* Pepperoni Pizza

SERVES 4

1 quantity Bread Dough Base (see page 156)
1 tbsp olive oil
1 tbsp freshly grated Parmesan
1 quantity Special Tomato Sauce
   (see page 160)
1 cup diced lightly smoked bacon
½ green bell pepper, halved, seeded, and
   thinly sliced
½ yellow bell pepper, halved, seeded, and
   thinly sliced
2 oz/55 g pepperoni-style sliced spicy
   sausage
½ cup smoked Bavarian cheese, grated
½ tsp dried oregano
olive oil, for drizzling
salt and pepper

1 Roll out or press the dough, using a rolling pin or your hands, into a
10-inch/25-cm circle on a lightly floured counter.

2 Place the dough base on a large greased cookie sheet or pizza pan and push
up the edge a little with your fingers, to form a rim.

3 Brush the base with the olive oil and sprinkle with the Parmesan. Cover and
leave to rise slightly in a warm place for about 10 minutes.

4 Spread the Special Tomato Sauce over the base almost to the edge. Top with
the bacon and bell peppers. Arrange the pepperoni on top and sprinkle with
the smoked cheese.

5 Sprinkle over the oregano and drizzle with a little olive oil. Season well.

6 Bake in a preheated oven, at 400°F/200°C, for 18–20 minutes, or until the
crust is golden and crisp around the edge. Cut the pizza into wedges and
serve immediately.

NUTRITION
Calories *450*; Sugars *6 g*; Protein *19 g*;
Carbohydrate *41 g*; Fat *24 g*; Saturates *6 g*

moderate

1 hr 30 mins

20 mins

This pizza is topped with a cocktail of mixed seafood, such as shrimp, mussels, cockles and squid rings.

Marinara Pizza

1 Roll out or press out the potato dough, using a rolling pin or your hands, into a 10-inch/25-cm circle on a lightly floured work surface.

2 Place the dough on a large greased cookie sheet or pizza pan and push up the edge a little with your fingers to form a rim.

3 Spread the tomato sauce evenly over the base almost to the edge.

4 Arrange the seafood cocktail, capers, and yellow bell pepper on top of the tomato sauce.

5 Sprinkle over the herbs and cheeses. Arrange the olives on top. Drizzle over a little olive oil and season with salt and pepper to taste.

6 Bake in a preheated oven, at 400°F/200°C, for 18–20 minutes or until the edge of the pizza is crisp and golden brown.

7 Transfer to a warmed serving plate, garnish with a sprig of marjoram or oregano and serve immediately.

SERVES 4

1 quantity Potato Base (see page 158)
1 quantity Special Tomato Sauce (see page 160)
7 oz/200 frozen seafood cocktail, thawed
1 tbsp capers
1 small yellow bell pepper, halved, seeded, and chopped
1 tbsp chopped fresh marjoram
½ tsp dried oregano
½ cup grated mozzarella cheese
1 tbsp grated Parmesan cheese
12 black olives
olive oil, for drizzling
salt and pepper
sprig of fresh marjoram or oregano, to garnish

NUTRITION
Calories *359*; Sugars *9 g*; Protein *19 g*; Carbohydrate *42 g*; Fat *14 g*; Saturates *4 g*

   moderate
2 hrs 30 mins
20 mins

🖫 **COOK'S TIP**

You can use a selection of fresh seafood for this pizza. If available, use peeled shrimp, cooked squid, shelled mussels and cockles.

This is a French variation of the classic Italian pizza, but is made with ready-made puff pie dough. It is perfect for outdoor eating.

Pissaladière

SERVES 4

butter, for greasing
4 tbsp olive oil
1 lb 9 oz/700 g red onions, thinly sliced
2 garlic cloves, crushed
2 tsp superfine sugar
2 tbsp red wine vinegar
12 oz/350 g ready-made puff pie dough,
   thawed if frozen
salt and pepper

topping
3 ½ oz/100 g canned anchovy fillets
12 green pitted olives
1 tsp dried marjoram

1 Lightly grease an edged cookie sheet. Heat the oil in a large pan. Cook the onions and garlic over low heat for about 30 minutes, stirring occasionally.

2 Add the sugar and red wine vinegar to the pan and season with plenty of salt and pepper.

3 On a lightly floured counter, roll out the pie dough to a rectangle measuring about 13 x 9 inches/33 x 23 cm. Carefully transfer the dough rectangle to the prepared cookie sheet, pushing the dough well into the corners.

4 Spread the onion mixture evenly over the dough.

5 Arrange the anchovy fillets in a criss-cross pattern on top, dot with the green olives, then sprinkle with the dried marjoram.

6 Bake in a preheated oven, 425°F/220°C, for 20–25 minutes, until the pissaladière is lightly golden. Serve piping hot, straight from the oven.

NUTRITION

Calories *612*; Sugars *13 g*; Protein *12 g*;
Carbohydrate *47 g*; Fat *43 g*; Saturates *11 g*

easy

20 mins

55 mins

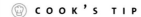 COOK'S TIP

Cut the pissaladière into squares or triangles for easy-to-eat finger food at a party or barbecue.

These pizza dough Italian pasties are best served hot with a salad for a delicious lunch or supper dish.

Potato *and* Tomato Calzone

1 To make the dough, strain the flour into a large mixing bowl and stir in the yeast. Make a well in the center of the mixture. Stir in the vegetable bouillon, honey, and caraway seeds, and slowly bring the mixture together to form a dough.

2 Turn the dough out on to a lightly floured counter and knead for 8 minutes until smooth. Place the dough in a lightly oiled mixing bowl, then cover and leave to rise in a warm place for 1 hour or until it has doubled in size.

3 Meanwhile, make the filling. Heat the oil in a skillet and add all the remaining ingredients except for the cheese. Cook for about 5 minutes, stirring occasionally.

4 Divide the risen dough into 4 pieces. On a lightly floured counter, roll them out to form four 7-inch/18-cm circles. Spoon equal amounts of the filling on to one half of each circle. Sprinkle the cheese over the filling. Brush the edges of the dough with milk and fold the dough over to form 4 semi-circles, pressing to seal the edges.

5 Place on a non-slip cookie sheet and brush with milk. Cook in a preheated oven, 425°F/220°C, for 30 minutes, until golden and risen.

SERVES 4

dough
4 cups white bread flour
1 tsp rapid-rise dry yeast
1 ¼ cups vegetable bouillon, warm
1 tbsp clear honey
1 tsp caraway seeds
skim milk, for glazing

filling
1 tbsp vegetable oil
1 ⅓ cups diced waxy potatoes
1 onion, halved and sliced
2 garlic cloves, crushed
1 ½ oz/40 g sun-dried tomatoes
2 tbsp chopped fresh basil
2 tbsp tomato paste
2 celery stalks, sliced
½ cup grated mozzarella cheese

NUTRITION
Calories *524*; Sugars *8 g*; Protein *17 g*;
Carbohydrate *103 g*; Fat *8 g*; Saturates *2 g*

  moderate

  1 hr 30 mins

35 mins

Index